C000218800

THE STA'
BLACK Bkɪɪ ʌɪɪʋ

Volume One

by Dr Aaron Haynes

*Dedicated to the memory
of my beloved mother
Charlotte*

First published in 1983 by
Root Publishing Co Limited
This New Edition published in 1996 by
Hansib Publishing (Caribbean) Ltd
P O Box 2773, St John's, Antigua, West Indies

Printed in the United Kingdom by
Martins the Printers Limited, Berwick Upon Tweed
Distributed by
Readers Book Club (Books Direct)
Third Floor, Tower House, 141-149 Fonthill Road
London N4 3HF England

ISBN 976-8163-01-1

CONTENTS

FOREWORD

THE STATE OF BLACK BRITAIN first appeared in 1983, in the aftermath of the urban disturbances of 1981. It added a welcome insight into the debate about race relations in Britain from a black perspective and shifted the agenda from that being established by the Scarman Report which was essentially about police/community relations, institutional racism and positive discrimination. Those issues were controversial then, as they are now, but the heat generated by the discussions led to more marginal programmes, much more paper policies on equal opportunities and limited real gains for ethnic minorities as a whole in Britain.

Aaron Haynes, in updating this volume, has the advantage of 13 years additional experience of race and social policies affecting ethnic and power relationships in a rapidly changing British society. Those changes are as responsive to the structural movements occurring in the domestic and world economies as well as in response to shifting patterns of global cultural diversity.

THE STATE OF BLACK BRITAIN not only provides a useful historical basis of where we were and how we got here, but contributes both to the thinking of what needs to be done and how, in order to contribute to the making of a just society in which everyone has an equal chance to learn, live and work free from racial prejudice and discrimination and free from the fear of racial harassment and violence.

Herman Ouseley
Chairman
Commission for Racial Equality
11 June 1996

PREFACE

The street disturbances of 1981 have had the effect of heightening the public debate on race relations in many circles throughout Britain. Despite the Scarman Report there has been a tendency to concentrate on treating the symptoms rather than the causes and there is a serious danger that developing improved police techniques for dealing with street violence will take precedence over removing the blatant inequalities in our society.

The State of Black Britain: The Failure of Official Race Relations Policy, is designed to give administrators and policy makers at all levels in the public and private sectors a concise review of the issues underlying the development of the present plight of Black people in Britain. It would be helpful to a wide range of practitioners, professionals and students who seek an understanding of the realities of the implications of various public policies for Black families. It can be used as a handbook for the uninitiated coming to race relations for the first time.

Apart from passing references, the book does not deal at any length with police-black community relations nor with the media, which I propose to develop in subsequent volumes dealing with these two vital areas of concern.

I would be amiss if I did not thank my many friends and colleagues who discussed various aspects of the issues raised in the book and contributed greatly to my conclusions. I am deeply indebted to Miss Beryl Cooper for patiently typing the manuscript and to my colleague and friend Bernard Gibbs and my wife Anita for sharing the arduous task of proof-reading.

Aaron Haynes

"Politicians continue talking about an 'immigration problem' when the real issue, ignored for more than a decade, is a deteriorating pattern of race relations."

Time "Underclass in the making"
20 August 1979

Chapter 1
An Introduction to the State of Black Britain

SIGNS OF ENTRENCHMENT

Although the presence of Black* people in Britain dates back to the times of the Romans, the post World War II presence that brought a steady flow of Black Commonwealth citizens to Britain[1] has posed a number of social, political and economic questions which need careful examination from the viewpoint of the Black man himself.

Britain was not the only European country to receive a post-war influx of Black citizens. Belgium, France and the Netherlands, all imperial powers with a colonial tradition, accepted during this period a number of Blacks settlers from their former colonies.[2] One substantial difference between the immigration to Continental European Countries and Britain was that whereas 90 per cent of the immigrant workers in the EEC area came from within the community or the Mediterranean and were therefore white migrants[3] more than half of Britain's immigrants were from the Asian subcontinent or the West Indies and were Black British subjects.[4] Only the Netherlands of the EEC countries had a ratio approaching that of Britain. In 1975 there were an estimated 120,000 Surinamese compared with an approximate quarter of a million white migrant workers and their families.[5] Against this background it is easy to see how the term "immigrant" came to mean "Black" in common usage in Britain and how the British political response to Blacks and their needs became confused with the response to immigration. Many Black people had hoped when emigrating to Britain from their native lands that they would have found ready acceptance for themselves and their children in the "mother country". They had been nurtured to see in British society the guardians of the rule of law, the custodians of justice and a Christian society, built on tolerance and charity towards strangers. They did

5

not expect to find a society hostile to Blacks and one in which racial discrimination would be prevalent.[6]

Soon they were to discover that the twin pressures of racial discrimination and their newness to the sophisticated social and economic system would operate as a clamp upon their aspirations and that few would break through the barriers except with great difficulty. As their numbers grew, and their plight worsened, they were subjected to one inquiry after another by white society, each confirming the growing spiral of deprivation, but oftimes concluding with the rhetoric of hope which has never found expression in their later experiences.

Between the mid-1950s and 1978 Black Britain grew from less than half a million to just about two million, i.e. from 1 per cent to 3.5 per cent of the total population.[7] Throughout these three decades there has been virtually no change in the socio-economic conditions and geographical location of Black people and a considerable deterioration for a section of young Blacks that has become a cause for great concern.

What is worse, however, is that Black Britain has begun to show signs of entrenchment at the bottom of the socio-economic ladder and this at a time when successive Governments have passed legislation designed to eliminate racial discrimination and promote equality of opportunity for Blacks. The Government White Paper on Racial Discrimination in 1975 states that:

> *"Beyond the problems of cultural alien-ness, there are the problems of low status, of material and environmental deprivation which involved immigrants and, increasingly, their children's experience to the extent that they share all or some of their problems with other groups in society, a general attack on deprivation will be relevant to their problems".*[8]

THE CRUCIAL QUESTIONS

Undoubtedly there is a wide gap between government policy and the fulfilment of Black needs. White institutions, whether they be private or public, are failing to respond sensitively to the Black presence and many well meaning people still point to the progress made by previous settlements of white immigrants, especially the Jews and Irish as evidence that Britain's Blacks, if only they would be patient, would one day break through the barrier. But is this true?

That indeed is the central question to which this study directs itself, for it is important to know whether in fact, time, nature's nurse, will heal the wounds inflicted on the Black community and whether like the white groups that preceded them they will

6

overcome the zenophobia of British society and achieve adequate upward mobility. The study will address itself to five areas:– the economic, educational, housing, social welfare and political.

The state of Black Britain has worried politicians and others alike for over two decades now. White Britain has never been able to perceive of itself as being a society dominated by racial discrimination.

A vigorous immigration policy aimed at controlling Black immigrants has been the constant position of successive governments. Over the past twenty years the debate has been almost exclusively of immigration. The 1948 British Nationality Act gave right of entry to Britain with the right of abode to every British subject including hundreds of millions of citizens of former colonial territories. Within a short period, however, three pieces of legislation (1962, 1968 and 1971) progressively changed this open-door immigration policy to one the consequences of which, in the words of a former Leader of the Inner London Education Authority, has been "to exclude those from English speaking countries with black or brown faces . . . ."[9].

The cumulative effect of this dramatic shift in immigration control was hardly intended to inspire confidence in Britain's Black communities either that they were welcomed in Britain or that their contribution to the society was valued. But, indeed, even the race and community relations lobby has itself been caught up in the belief that if only the government could get its immigration control right, then they would have a better chance of achieving racial harmony.

Over the same period three other pieces of legislation (1965, 1968 and 1976) have sought to eliminate racial discrimination and promote equality of opportunity. But despite this two pronged attack of racial harmony and equality of opportunity the Select Committee on Race Relations and Immigration, during 1968-69, demonstrated that over a wide range of problems there was need for concern at the experiences of young Black school leavers.[10]

In 1969 E.J.B. Rose in Colour and Citizenship wrote:

"The concentration of coloured immigrants in certain sections of employment and their absence in others, coupled with the fact that there has been little or no change between 1961 and 1966 gives most cause for concern".

Then he goes on to warn:

"If this pattern continues into the 1970s then the assessment that this situation is still fluid and has not hardened into a rigid class-colour or caste-colour structure may well be over-optimistic".[12]

7

However, in 1974 a survey conducted by the Community Relations Commission revealed that Black (especially West Indian) youths were twice as likely to be unemployed as their indigenous counterparts.[13] Indeed David Smith's studies showed that for West Indians alone it was four times as difficult for a young West Indian school leaver to get a job than his white counterpart.[14] At the height of the recession in 1980 the rate of increase of unemployment among young Blacks was four times that of their white counterparts.

In the field of housing the picture is equally depressing. Whether in private or public housing, Black Britain finds itself in the least desirable end of the housing market and oftimes has to pay what is later described as a "colour tax" for the privilege of being at the bottom. The question that will need to be resolved is how can Black Britain break out of this housing stranglehold?

What has been described as the "immigrant syndrome" that is the community pressures which constitute a significant "pull" factor especially amongst those who wish to withdraw from British social life, mainly because they are not fluent in English or because they are in a strange environment, is sometimes offered as a reason not only for Black Britain's plight in housing but also consequentially in education. In the final analysis this notion must be carefully examined in the light of the experiences of other groups of settlers notably the Jews, Poles and Hungarians.

Since education is crucial to the ultimate advancement of any community the role of education in the state of Black Britain cannot be ignored. Of all groups, the educationists have been the most adamant in resisting any attempts to explore the extent of racial discrimination and the way it functions at the various levels of their service, yet throughout official thinking on the subject there are deep-seated prejudices which flow from the liberal academic lobby. The Commonwealth Immigrant Advisory Council, set up in 1963, in its Second Report, states that one of the disadvantages of concentration of pupils from ethnic minority groups – a euphemism for blacks – is that it impairs the progress of indigenous (white) pupils by interrupting the normal routine of school. But it went further than that and added:

"There is a further danger that educational backwardness which, in fact is due to environment, language or a different culture, may increasingly be supposed to arise from some inherent or genetic infirmity".[15]

Later, Sir Edward Boyle in explaining his now notorious Circular in which local authorities were admonished to restrict the number of immigrant children in any one school, told the House of Commons; "I must respectfully tell the House that one school must be regarded now as inevitably an immigrant school. The important thing to do is to prevent this happening elsewhere".[16]

A further justification for this study comes in the response of a policy maker in the social services department of one local authority which is by no means atypical. He said: "I personally do not think that this borough has either the expertise or the resources to fully work through some of the needs and their implications among ethnic minority groups. I'm not quite sure that if we even had all the money we require, we would know where to begin, where to start and what's required".[17] The real question now must be: how far can Black Britain help resolve that dilemma?

The social services is the point at which all the disadvantaged meet and it is likely because of that fact to be a service where the case for special needs can be made and accepted. But if one fails here, where is the hope? While because of the make-up of Black Britain it has so far made less of a demand on the social services of the nation, such demands as it has made have been poorly met. As self-support from within the community has broken down with the collapse of the extended family, more and more demands have been put on the service that has shown itself unprepared.

The first Wilson government in response to all this swiftly created two bodies. The Race Relations Board (1965) was given the task of leading the fight against racial discrimination and the National Committee for Commonwealth Immigrants (1965), through a network of local organisations, would seek through public education and persuasion to promote racial harmony and equality of opportunity and to achieve attitude change. This latter body became the Community Relations Commission in 1968 and the two were eventually merged into the Commission for Racial Equality in 1977, as a result of the Race Relations Act 1976. The effectiveness of these institutions needs to be assessed as part of the political response to Black Britain.

In addition while government accepted in theory the principle of central government funding to meet the needs of multi-racial areas in general, there was little commitment to funding multi-racial groups until comparatively quite recently. In consequence both the Urban Aid Programme (Local Government Grants (Social Need) Act of 1969) whose origin and design was justified as an instrument to help areas with, among other things, heavy concentrations of

9

Blacks; and Section 11 of the Local Government Act (1966) which provided assistance to help authorities meet the special needs of immigrants, have done little to relieve the disadvantages faced by the black communities.

The ambivalence of government was illustrated by two statements associated with the transfer of the Urban Programme from the Home Office to the Department of the Environment in a rationalisation of Inner City policy. The first came from the Minister of State responsible for the programme, Peter Shore, in the House of Commons on April 6, 1977. It was a clear statement that the programme was not directed at multi-racial issues:

> *"My purpose is to deal, regardless of whether there are black or white populations, with aggregated problems of poverty and deprivation in our major urban centres".*[18]

The second comes in the White Paper *Policy for the Inner Cities*, published in June 1977, and states: "the Government intends to require that the needs of the ethnic minorities are fully taken into account in the planning and implementation of policies of the inner city areas, and in the allocation of resources under the enlarged programme".[19] It did not say how the Government proposed to do this, but added "local authorities will, therefore, need to ensure that, when they put forward proposals in this context, the needs of ethnic minorities are taken fully into account".[20]

It is important throughout this study to examine who determines what solutions are going to be tried in attempts to meet the needs of Black Britain, and how wide is the gulf between theory and practice, promise and reality, Black needs and service fulfilment.

Despite pious statements none of the major political parties has so far been bold enough to put forward a Black candidate in a safe parliamentary seat, but analysis of the Black voting patterns demonstrated that in the 1974 election, the Black vote was critical to the Labour Party's success. At local authority level there has been a slow but steady increase in the number of Black local councillors being elected and the 1979 General Election saw these councillors attempt, for the first time, the formation of a Black Caucus. This development is important to this study as it signals the beginning of a political initiative which will need to be looked at in relation to issues such as police/Black relations, the law and order theme and related matters.

It is clear that in so far as successive governments were concerned the overall strategy was two-pronged. On the one hand there was the goal of racial harmony which was pursued on the assumption that a rigorous immigration policy would limit the growth of the Black community to acceptable levels of social integration. On the other hand the pursuit of equality of opportunity through the elimination of racial discrimination would promote upward mobility for Blacks. Those responsible for the first prong pursued their objective with almost ecclesiastical zeal, while those responsible for the second prong often found themselves hampered by a complex mixture of their own uncertainty, lack of genuine Government commitment, the white backlash and poor community organisation in the Black communities themselves.

In addition it is only within the last five years that Governments have given any recognition to Black self-help and made any attempt to consult the Black community itself on its needs and the way in which those needs might be met. How Blacks meet this new situation will determine to a large measure the course of the future. Indeed the Parliamentary Select Committee on Race Relations and Immigration in its recent report on the West Indian community conceded the need for the Black community to have its own independent, collective, articulate voice.[21] The question that will certainly have to be answered is how will the experiences of the past act as a dampener on such a development.

Yet without it, official overall strategy in race and community relations will not achieve its stated objectives of harmony and equality of opportunity for Blacks. In the present state of Black Britain, racial discrimination is the major factor which inhibits development, and until this is realised a process which has already begun, will move unchecked to a Britain of "two nations" separate and unequal, the one black the other white.

THE GREAT GAP
The present state of Black Britain is a grim and unpleasant one, but an understanding of the issues, coupled with commitment to effect a fundamental change in policy directions on the part of both white institutions and Black organisations could substantially improve the quality of life in Britain and lead to a more integrated and equal society. In this respect it is worth noting the challenge set out in the White Paper, *Racial Discrimination,* when it said: "It is inconceivable that Britain in the last quarter of the Twentieth Century, should confess herself unable to secure for a small minority of around a million and a half coloured citizens, their full and equal rights as individual men and women."[22]

11

It is important to stress the great gap between Government's belief in its stated objectives and the real world outside. The White Paper states quite emphatically: "It is the Government's duty to prevent morally unacceptable and socially devisive inequalities from hardening into extended patterns". That excellently worded official statement was made fully over a decade after the results of the Political and Economic Planning report which examined the extent of racial discrimination in Britain were made public. In that report we are told: "racial discrimination varied in extent from the massive to the substantial",[23] but the report also states: "the experiences of white immigrants, such as Hungarians and Cypriots, compared to Black and brown immigrants, such as West Indians and Asians leave no doubt that the major component in the discrimination is colour. It is moreover, impossible to escape the conclusion that the more different a person is in his physical characteristics, in his features, in the texture of his hair and in the colour of his skin, the more discrimination he will face."[24] In a speech in Walsall on February 9, 1968, the Rt Hon Enoch Powell, then MP for Wolverhampton SW, had this to say of the failure to halt Black immigration into Britain:–

"Some problems are unavoidable. Some evils can be coped with to a certain extent but not prevented. But that the nation should have saddled itself without necessity and without counter-vailing benefit with a wholly avoidable problem of immense dimensions is enough to make one weep. That the same nation stubbornly persists in allowing the problem, great as it already is, to be magnified further, is enough to make one despair."

He followed this up with a speech in Birmingham on April 20 of the same year. On that occasion he was opposing the 1968 Race Relations Bill. He said:–

"There could be no grosser misconception of the realities than is entertained by those who vociferously demand legislation as they call it "against discrimination". They have got it exactly diametrically wrong. The discrimination and the deprivation, the sense of alarm and resentment, lies not with the immigrant population, but with those among whom they have come and are still coming. This is why to enact legislation of the kind before Parliament at this moment is to risk throwing a match on to gunpowder. The kindest thing that can be said about those who propose and support it is that they know not what they do".

He then added his most popular prophecy of the prospect of racial conflict: "As I look ahead, I am filled with foreboding. Like the

12

Roman, I see the River Tiber foaming with much blood". Making the point that Powell was representative of a much wider malaise, Dr Stuart Hall, Director of the Centre for Cultural Studies, Birmingham University, wrote:

"By 'Powellism' I mean something larger and more significant than the enunciation of a specifically defiant policy about race and the Black population by a single person. I mean the formation of an 'official' racial politics at the heart of British political culture".[25]

The frustration of thousands of Blacks can be summed up in the words of Orville Byron, a young man who came to England from his native West Indies. He gave expression to his experience and that of thousands of his peer group in these terms:

"I thought the people would be friendly because in the West Indies white and Black get along very well, so I thought to myself there will be no problem. This was shattered in a few weeks, and the dreams of making it in the Mother Country were gone, not for a while, but forever".[26]

Time, the international weekly news magazine in an article written by their European team and published on August 20 1979, had this to say:

"Politicians continue talking about an 'immigration problem' when the real issue, ignored for more than a decade, is a deteriorating pattern of race relations"[27]

and after recounting the clash between the police and the Asian community in Southall during the general election campaign of the Spring 1979, it added:

"The clash was fresh evidence, if any more were needed, that Britain's race problem is growing worse as new generations of more self-confident black and brown citizens come of age, determined to demand their rights in ways their parents never dared. The Government behaves as if time and good intentions will somehow prevail over racial conflict and most Britons are simply unprepared to deal with the challenge of adapting to a multi-racial society. There is, in fact, an almost unconscious refusal to accept that reality."[28]

The same article cites two interesting views of Britain's approach to racism. One by a ranking civil servant:

"I think the difference between the United States and here is that in America the Government has been willing to do something more than pass laws. Here, Government has done as little as possible. Once Parliament had passed the Race Relations Act,

13

it then treated it as a bed to sleep on".[29]

The other by India-born Dr Bikhu Parekh, senior lecturer in politics at University of Hull, who said:

"English racism was calm, arrogant, secure in its self-righteousness and self-confidence".[30]

Bridging the gap between official good intentions and the country's unwillingness to come to terms with the demands of a pluralist society will call for considerable reserves of character of both mind and spirit. Gone are the days when Britain ruled the waves. Gone are the glorious days of imperial power when the Empire stretched from one end of the globe to the other. But present is one golden hour in which to demonstrate to the rest of the world that mankind is not only capable of reaching the moon, but also of achieving a level of human understanding that would make a genuine multi-racial society, not the faded dream of a few, but the living experience of all.

"Right now the trade union movement in Britain is functioning as a white man's union and thus must be challenged. In challenging this we believe in the unity of the working class. This unity must be solidly established indeed and not only in words. It is the main task of the trade union movement to create this unity".

Amrit Wilson. *Finding a Voice*
London, Virago 1978, page 59

Chapter 2

Promised Land or Economic Wilderness

THE EMPLOYED

When the majority of Blacks came to Britain, they did so convinced that they would be able to improve their economic plight and thus offer their children not only a higher standard of living than they themselves had enjoyed, but also an enhanced quality of life.

The job opportunities opened to them have therefore been crucial in determining whether or not that dream would be fulfilled. Against the push factor for them to emigrate to Britain, there was also the pull factor of Britain's own need for manpower to meet the demand of a labour-intensive industrial complex and of people to fill the lower-paid service jobs vacated by white workers in the post-war years.

Once here they set about finding themselves jobs, and employment among these first generation immigrants was high largely because they were by and large of working age and because they were prepared to accept whatever came their way in the form of employment. A dirty and low paid job in England was better than no job at all in their country of origin, and even those among them who did not obtain jobs commensurate with their qualifications still often found themselves in a better position to care for the material needs of their families back home than if they had not emigrated. They thus endured their plight in the hope that their children would do better. Few of them, conditioned as they were to believing in the justice, fairplay and tolerance of British society, even suspected that their status and job level was being determined by the prejudices which the society harboured against blacks. And indeed, their white liberal friends kept pointing to how well immigrant groups who had preceded them had succeeded and that with time their children would make up the lost ground.

Extracts from the General Household Survey for 1972 reveal that 91% of ethnic minority men compared with 77% of white men are working over all ages. However, if we study those aged 16-54 we find that 93% of ethnic minority men and 91% of white men are working. Similarly turning our attention to women and looking only at West Indian women as compared with white women, the same source reveals that 74% of West Indian women as against 43% of all women are working and that the difference is greatest in the child-bearing ages of 25-44. Confining our attention to the 16-54 age groups 75% of West Indians compared with 55% of the general female population are working. There are marked differences between non-Moslem Asian and Moslem Asian women as between Asian and West Indian women as set out below:

Table 1
Proportion of West Indian and Asian women who are working

% of each age group who are working

	West Indian	Non-Moslem Asians	Moslem Asians	All Women
Women of all ages	74	45	17	43
Women 16-54	75	47	18	55

Table 2
Proportion of West Indian and all women who are working

% of each age group who are working

	West Indian Women	All Women	Difference
Women of all ages	74	43	31
16-24	57	55	02
25-34	73	44	29
35-44	83	58	25
45-54	77	63	14
16-54	75	55	20

Black women also found it necessary to work to a greater extent than their white counterparts. It is difficult to escape the conclusion of the Thomas Cowan Unit at the Institute of

16

Education that in the case of West Indian women the high percentage to be found at work is a matter of necessity rather than choice. Facilities and arrangements for chid-care while they are at work leave much to be desired and more often than not, are completely lacking. Two factors appear to be operative here. One, the low status jobs of West Indian males require the supplement of the female income to manage the family budget; and second, the higher proportion of one-parent families within the West Indian community often leaves the woman as the sole bread winner.

Even Moslem women have found it necessary to work despite the difficulties of finding jobs where their cultural norms can be respected. One in five Moslem Asian women is at work and that is against four in five for West Indian women and one in two of non-Moslem Asian women.

Black Britain has clearly been prepared to work, but as Cross made clear in his study of "Ethnic Minorities in the Inner City" there is both a racial and sexual element in the way in which jobs have been made available to members of the black community, and the pattern which has emerged gives credence to the concept of ethnic minority workers being the "new proletariat".

A great deal of concern has been shown in the sorts of jobs which blacks do as compared with their white counterparts. Here the reports consistently show an under-representation of blacks in the clerical and professional occupations and an over-representation in labouring jobs with degrees of regional variation. Cross points out that –

"In the West Midlands, one-fifth of the males of each New Commonwealth group are labourers, but this proportion rises to one-half for Pakistanis, most of whom work in engineering and allied trades. Indian-born females are well represented in clerical and professional jobs in the London area, and West Indian women in service occupations while Cypriot females are largely in the clothing trade."[1]

He sums up the situation by saying –

"This pattern of status distribution provides considerable substance for those who have referred to ethnic minority workers as the new proletariat but one which is distinguishable by its colour and which undertakes a wide range of employment activities which their indigenous counterparts do not wish to undertake as; living standards rise."[2]

The PEP reports confirm this picture showing male Africans and

17

Asians as over-represented and West Indians under-represented in clerical and professional occupations in the London area when compared with indigenous whites, whereas in the Midlands all male workers especially Pakistanis are over-represented amongst the labourers.[3]

David Smith in his study, shows that the job levels of Asian and West Indian men are substantially lower than those of white men. The gap between Pakistanis and white being the widest with West Indians coming next. Indians after these and that between African-Asians and whites being comparatively small.[4] The results of his study are set out in Table 3.

Table 3
Job Level Analysis by Country of Origin – Men

Job Level/Socio Economic Group 1	White	West Indian	Pakistani/ Bangladeshi	Indian	African Asian
	%	%	%	%	%
Professional/ Management	23) 40	2) 8	4) 8	8) 20	10) 30
White Collar	17)	6)	4)	12)	20)
Skilled Manual	42	59	33	44	44
Semi-skilled Manual	12)	23)	38)	27)	24)
	6)	9)	20)	9)	2)
Not Classified	1	1	1		

Smith, D. Racial Disadvantage in Britain. PEP. London 1971, page 73

It is tragic, and a matter of grave concern that Black Britain has begun to show signs of entrenchment at the bottom of the socio-economic ladder. Throughout the last two decades there has been virtually no change in the relative socio-economic conditions and status location of Black people generally, but what is worse is the considerable deterioration for a section of young Blacks. Many Black parents who had turned to Britain as the "Promised Land" with a bright future for their children, still dream for that future, but are beginning to question whether it has not instead been a journey into the wilderness.

Generally speaking, therefore, the statistics show that a higher percentage of both men and women from amongst Britain's ethnic minorities are working when compared with their white counterparts.

Dr Crispin Cross, pointing to the importance of employment says:–

> *"It could be argued, and with considerable justification, that the issue of unemployment is the most critical determinant of the state of community relations in the country as a whole, as well as in the conurbations where most ethnic minority members have settled. This is because it is bound up with the daily basis of life of the community as a whole and with the expectations of members of ethnic minority communities who decided to settle in those areas where they could find employment. It is also crucially important because it clearly reflects the attitudes of the host community to immigrants who seek employment in order to maintain themselves and their families."*[5]

There are two other pieces of evidence that are important here. The first is that when it comes to professional/managerial jobs even where Blacks have the necessary qualifications they find it difficult to break through to those areas of responsibility. In contrast white workers can expect, even without formal qualifications, to rise up through the ranks and attain these positions. This has resulted in a number of academically qualified Blacks being forced into doing manual jobs, and a disincentive to young Blacks to put in the effort necessary to attain qualifications. The fact that where Blacks have the necessary qualifications for skilled manual jobs they do almost as well as their white counterparts points strongly to the conclusion that the prejudice experienced by Blacks in attaining top status jobs in British society is heavily tinted by class.

When Smith went on to examine the relationship between job level and degree standard qualifications he found that 79 per cent of white men with degrees were in professional or managerial jobs, compared with only 31 per cent of Black men and that while there were none of the white men doing manual jobs of any kind, 21 per cent of Black men with degree qualifications were doing such jobs. Similar comparisons at other levels of educational qualification though less stark are still strong and illustrate that while white people without formal qualifications may still rise through the ranks to professional and managerial jobs, this is well nigh impossible for Blacks. Where, however, Blacks have the qualifications for skilled manual jobs they are in near equality with whites.[6]

The correlation between educational qualifications and job level will be discussed later, but it would suffice here to note the Smith results, especially the barriers to access in respect of high status jobs.

Table 4
Job levels of men with degree standard qualifications
White and Minority men compared

	White Men %	Minority Men %
Professional/Management	79	31
White Collar	22	48
Skilled Manual	–	14
Semi-skilled Manual	–	04
Unskilled Manual	–	03

Smith, D. *Racial Disadvantage in Britain*. PEP London 1977, page 75.

The second is that it is twice as likely for a Black worker to be working on some form of shift system as his white counterpart and three times as likely that he would be on a permanent night shift. It has been shown also that despite some night shifts being predominantly made up of Black workers, the chances of one of them becoming foreman is not great. Indeed in many instances Black night shift workers are passed over for promotion so that the only white workers on night shifts are the supervisors.

Smith went on to analyse the frequency of Black workers in the intrinsically undesirable shiftwork system and found that 27 per cent of Pakistani men compared with 9 per cent of white men were working some kind of night shift and that indeed they were more likely to be working permanent night shift. Even when account was taken of the under-representation of Black workers in the higher job levels and the over-representation in the lower levels, Smith found that even if white men were distributed between job levels in the same way as Black, then only 21 per cent of white men compared with 31 per cent of Black men would be expected to work shift work.[7]

Table 5
Shiftwork by Country of Origin in Men

Types of Shift	Whites %	Minor- ities %	West Indians %	Pakistani/ Bangladeshi %	Indian %	African %
Permanent Nights	1	3	1	8	4	3
Total Night Shifts	9	19	19	27	18	12
Day Shifts	5	12	13	11	12	9
Total Working Shifts	15	31	31	38	30	30

Smith, David. Op cit, page 81

What the evidence does reveal is that British society not only under-values and under-uses its Black talent at all levels, and specifically at top level, but that this pattern is so entrenched as to leave young Blacks with few models of success and achievement. It thus reinforces a sense of inadequacy and inferiority. So that while it is true that a large percentage of Black Britain is at work, they are occupied in the dirty, low status, dead-end jobs which whites no longer want, with a disproportionate number of their women in non-unionised near-sweat-shop conditions of the rag trade.

THE UNEMPLOYED

What has been even more disturbing, however, is the deepening trends towards unemployability among Black youth in general and West Indian youth in particular. Over the past fifteen years the plight of this group has become worse, and has been aggravated by each period of recession. Twelve years after the 1968 study by the Parliamentary Select Committee on Race and Immigration on the *Coloured School Leaver*, unemployment among young Black Britons is still running at three times the national average. This points to one thing – a failure of official strategy to stem the disproportionate growth of unemployment in the Black communities.

But unemployment among blacks is not a recent phenomenon.

Department of Employment statistics of February 1963, show that minority groups accounted for 6 per cent of those registered as unemployed, even at a time when these constituted only about 1½ per cent of the workforce.[8] However, the 1971 census data set unemployment among minorities at 7.2 per cent compared with 5.4 per cent for the general population, but it also pointed to two groups of Blacks – the young and women – who showed a marked difference when compared with white groups. In the age group up to 20 years, unemployment was nearly 20 per cent among girls born in West Indies, India and Pakistan, compared with 7 per cent for all girls in the same age group. Among West Indian boys of the same group the unemployment level was 17 per cent compared with 9 per cent for all boys in that age group.[9]

Table 6
Percentage of economically active who were unemployed, analysed by birth-place and age – 1971 Census

	Total	Age up to 20	21.25	26-35	36-55	56+
All men	5.4	8.6	6.0	4.6	4.2	6.8
Born in West Indies	7.7	16.9	12.5	6.8	6.2	8.8
India	5.3	6.9	5.4	4.0	5.1	8.5
Pakistan/ Bangladesh	5.8	7.4	6.0	4.6	56.	9.2
All women	5.6	7.3	5.3	5.7	4.6	6.6
Born in West Indies	9.5	18.3	9.6	8,8	8.0	9.9
India	8.7	13.8	11.6	9.3	7.0	7.0
Pakistan/ Bangladesh	13.1	22.6	14. 9	13. 7	9.4	7.3

Source: 1971 Census Advance Analysis

David Smith argues that "as the total unemployment rises, so the minorities tend to make up a greater proportion of this total" in other words, unemployment of minorities rises more steeply than total unemployment.[10] He adds that "if unemployment continues to rise we can expect the minorities to be put at an increasing relative disadvantage".[11] The Department of Employment statistics relative this view. As the economy plunged into recession in the mid-70s unemployment among all Black workers rose from 2.2 per cent of the national total in November 1973 to 3.4 per cent in May 1975, but more significantly the rate of increase was twice as large among Black female workers.[12] The recession of 1979/80 produced even more striking results as the rate of increase in Black youth unemployment reached as high as four times that for white youths and jobs in the hosiery and knitwear industries, traditionally held by Black female workers, were decimated.

Support for the correlation between recession and the worsening fortunes of Black workers is also found in Dennis Brooke's study of Walsall which dramatically describes the situation as folows: "When Britain sneezes, Walsall catches pneumonia – but Walsall's Black workers catch double pneumonia."[13]

In the 60s and early 70s the Asian community in the bigger cities had sought to cope with this problem through taking over a number of corner-shops which white proprietors were giving up upon their retirement because their sons and daughters no longer found them attractive propositions. By opening for long hours and much of the weekend at least some, if not all the members, of the household could be involved in the business. As children have grown older, these concerns have not been able to provide sufficient income to maintain full employment for all, and more and more Asian young people have been forced on to the traditional job market with the relative rapid increase in the rate of their unemployment.

EARNINGS

Despite the picture painted so far of the Black community trapped in the economic wilderness of low status jobs, low pay and with their children condemned to a mere continuation of their parents plight if not worse, there has been an estimate by the Afro-Caribbean Development Society of a gross weekly earnings by the Afro-Caribbeans in the labour force of some £40 millions in 1977. The estimate for the Asians in the labour force for the same year was £52 millions. But both are well below the national per capita average and fully reflect the consequences of job levels, shift-work and the age

23

and sex distribution on earning potential.

RECRUITMENT TRAINING and PROMOTION

The position of Blacks in the labour force is a cumulative function of three separate but inter-related processes in the use of manpower resources – recruitment, training and promotion. It has been shown how job levels of Blacks compare unfavourably with their white counterparts, and that even well qualified Blacks find difficulty in obtaining jobs commensurate with their qualifications and skills.

This is surely the result of defective recruitment policies and practices. What is amazing is that a personnel manager charged with the responsibility of securing for his firm the best in labour power resources, can afford to be so remiss without fear of consequences to his own security. No works manager or quality controller who was equally remiss in material control would survive in employment for long. It is easier in this case to waste or under-use human resources than to do the same with material resources.

But not only is the selection process at fault, so too are the procedures and principles underlying training and promotion, for all the evidence points to the failure of Black workers to do as well as their white counterparts in being granted in-service training and being afforded advancement through promotion.

The sheer complacency among employment circles as evidenced by the Canby and Thaken study for the Institute of Personnel Management is alarming. The study carried the very intriguing title "No Problems Here". It looked at the problems which typically arise in a multi-racial workforce and reflected the general lack of appreciation by many managers in their failure to meet the need of Black workers.

Managers are content to shelter behind "they are not coming forward" as a response for not having more Black employees or for not having trained or promoted a greater percentage of those they do have. Seldom do they seek to ask themselves: "Why are they not coming forward?" There are four reasons why they have not been asking themselves this vital question.

The first is that so far despite the statistical evidence, managers do not perceive the under-utilisation of Black labour power as a resource as a serious problem.

The second is that the race relations lobby has for years adopted an unrealistic do-gooding profile trying to sell equal opportunity as something good for Blacks rather than something good for business.

Businessmen are primarily concerned with the profitability and efficiency of their businesses not the wellbeing of Blacks. They will pursue the latter as a means to the former but not as an end in itself. However, the Code of Practice required under the Race Relations Act 1976, and published as a consultative document early in 1980, while retaining some of the moralistic arguments does put the issue within the framework of law and commercial practice. If finally approved by Parliament it is likely to have the effect of causing managers to give more serious thought to this matter.

The third reason is the attitude and status of Blacks themselves. While Blacks are aware of their failure to get recruited for certain jobs, as well as the lack of training opportunities and promotion prospects, they have not so far devised a collective response to this situation. This failure on their part will be dealt with later, but suffice it to say here that this lack of collective response has been interpreted by many as evidence that no problem exists. More important, however, is the status of Blacks. Until Blacks become employers in their own right there can be no hope for equality of opportunity in the employment field.

The fourth reason is the level of racial discrimination present in the society and which the society as a nation is prepared to accept. Whether consciously or unconsciously the decision-making process at each level of recruitment, training and promotion will be affected by the existing levels and forms of racial discrimination.

RACIAL DISCRIMINATION IN EMPLOYMENT

The most extensive evidence to date on the level of racial discrimination in employment is provided by a series of PEP reports based on work carried out between 1972 and 1975. This work was jointly financed by Gulbenkian Foundation and the Home Office, and later published with the assistance of Nuffield Foundation in one book *Racial Disadvantage in Britain*[14]. But PEP were not the only ones to establish this link between racial discrimination and the employment prospects of Blacks. Roger Ballard and Bronwen Holden of the Social Science Research Council (SSRC) Unit on Ethnic Relations at Bristol University, found that coloured university students who were born and educated in Britain were considerably disadvantaged in getting jobs commensurate with their qualifications when compared with their indigenous counterparts who had similar qualifications.[15]

Cross cites other evidence from a study by J.H. Taylor in Newcastle-upon-Tyne indicating that although some ethnic minority students may do as well as or better than their white

25

counterparts, they still experience similar difficulties in obtaining employment[16] and concludes "that 'employability' is not just a function of the skills possessed by candidates nor is it a function of the industrial or non-industrial nature of the backgrounds from which they derive."[17]

Indeed, Jowell and Prescott-Clarke found that there was a strong suspicion among adult immigrants that far from being a passport to a choice of employment, their educational qualifications often heightened the racial discrimination they experienced.[18]

The PEP and other reports have left no doubt as to the extent of racial discrimination in employment and that it represented a crucial factor in the job prospects for Blacks. But the subtle processes by which it took place made it extremely difficult for the victim, even when he sensed it was taking place, to prove it and oftimes left the victim exposed to being accused of carrying a chip on his shoulder.

Both the old Race Relations Board and the Commission for Racial Equality testify to the difficulty in getting the concrete evidence to sustain in a judicial forum the contention that an act of discrimination had taken place in the field of employment. This is even more so when the nature of the discrimination is indirect as opposed to direct discrimination.

The victims of discrimination are therefore faced with two problems. The first is identifying that discrimination has taken place from among the range of subtle and sophisticated devices open to the discriminator and the second is getting the evidence to establish the less favourable treatment to which the victim has been subjected.

White society has been reluctant to admit the existence of the current level of racial discrimination for to do so would be, for its members a betrayal of the standards of fair play, tolerance and justice for which the society prides itself. Yet all three of its major defences have fallen short of being convincing. The argument of "newness" would have suggested that second and third generations of Blacks, more accustomed to the demands of the industrial society in this country, would have done substantially better than their parents. The one issue about which all researchers are agreed is the underlying trend of worsening employment prospects for young Blacks.

The second defence theory is the poor command of the English language by Black workers. Many second generation Blacks now speak with an accent and usage of English indistinguishable from their white peers yet continue to do less well in the job stakes, and as

26

PEP points out it is among the educated Asians whose fluency in English is unquestioned that the disparity between the level of qualfication and the level of job attainment is most stark. The PEP survey not surprisingly concludes that:—

> "Language competence is unlikely to be a significant factor accounting for the comparatively low job levels of minority men with academic qualifications . . . there is a very strong relationship among Asians between fluency in English and academic qualifications, in fact, this relationship is so strong that nearly all Asian men with degree-equivalent qualifications speak English fluently. Yet it is among this very group that we find the greatest disparity between the level of qualifications and the level of the job".[19]

The third is in fact an extension of the other two and suggests that the increasingly better educated second and third generations would experience less difficulty in getting jobs, and be more eligible for promotion. The reality has been that those born and educated in Britain have found that their qualifications, while raising their expectations, have not guaranteed them jobs similar to their white counterparts. Indeed while the absence of qualifications provided the employer with a legitimate reason for refusing, having the qualification did not in itself offer a passport to employment.

It is not proposed to describe here the several strategems by which the discriminator accomplishes the exclusion of Black workers either from recruitment or training or promotion. It is clear, however, that in the face of the available evidence there is no logical explanation other than an unacceptable level of racial discrimination which can account for the current distribution of Blacks in the labour force.

THE TRADE UNION MOVEMENT and RACE

The Trade Union Movement was so ossified with its commitment to the "brotherhood of man" and the natural corollary of equality that followed from that concept, that the movement blindly asserted that the consideration of race was an irrelevance, even an affront, to Trade Union principles. Had the Trade Union Movement been alive to the needs of its Black members the disadvantages Blacks suffered, many of which have now become enshrined in practice, would never have occurred.

Time magazine reporting a TUC conference, quotes Bill Keys, – chairman of the TUC Equal Rights committee and at that time a member of the Commission for Racial Equality, as saying: "The

TUC was late at the gate as far as the racial question is concerned."[20]

The most stark expression of this is to be found in Amrit Wilson's discussion of Asian woman at work outside the home. In it one finds a description of the role of the Trades Union Movement in the disputes at Imperial Typewriters, Grunwick and Spiralynx, and vividly points out the difference between the struggles at Imperial and Spiralynx when compared with that at Grunwick. The author states emphatically:

"In fact, in many factories all over Britain, whites are not only on the side of trade union bureaucracy, but often on the side of the management against their Black workmates. But there has been a important exception. In the most important strike of 1976 and, 1977, the rank and file of the labour movement have demonstrated their support of Black workers."[21]

Then quoting from the Asian workers strike committee statement on the lesson of the Imperial Typewriter dispute, the author notes:–

"Our struggle has taught us also that Black workers must never for a moment entertain the thought of separate Black unions. They must join the existing unions and fight through them. Where the unions fail in their duties to Black workers they must be challenged to stand up for their rights. The union is an organisation of all workers, regardless of race, colour or sex. Right now the trade union movement in Britain is functioning as a white man's union and thus must be challenged. In challenging this we believe in the unity of the working class. This unity must be solidly established indeed and not only in words. It is the main task of the trade union movement to create this unity."[22]

Similarly, the Black workers in the dispute at Grunwick learned that they alone could not defeat their employers. They also saw that they and their white supporters were caught up in the trade union bureaucracy. Of this Amrit Wilson writes:

"At Grunwick this unity of the working class was achieved. Hundreds of trade unionists came day after day to support the Grunwick strikers on the picket line. But in the end it wasn't enough because they hadn't the courage to confront and defy the handful of men who control the trade union bureaucracy. The white working class had been weakened by their dependence on these leaders. They had grown unaccustomed to using their power of collective action. To remedy this weakness – that is the next task before the labour movement."[23]

What was noticeable, however, was the ease with which the National Association for Freedom, Grunwick boss George Ward (himself an Anglo-Asian) and the mass media were able to shift the emphasis away from the right of workers to join a union and the treatment of Black workers to a debate on the tools of working class struggle generally and the closed shop and picketting in particular.

The fact is that white trade union officials have colluded with white managements and their white members to maintain and preserve situations disadvantageous to their Black members. But it is not only in the field of advocacy and representation that the trade union movement has sold its Black members short. They have been neglected too in the area of training in trade unionism and in general advancement within the trade union movement. Not infrequently Black workers seeking to take industrial action have been denied the support of their white workmates and the trade union bureaucracy.

It is important to emphasize the two basic conclusions of the Asian workers strike committee in their statement on the lessons to be gained from the experience of the Imperial Typewriter strike. The first was that there is no mileage to be gained by Black workers contemplating separate Blacks only unions. The second was that where unions failed in their responsibilities to Black workers then there was a clear duty to challenge them.

Cross discusses the tendency to project antipathetic attitudes to other people and cites how this can even lead to connivance between management and trade unions in agreement to exclude Black workers from certain jobs and restricting their promotion on the supposition that white workers would find them unacceptable.[24] Both Department of Employment researchers[25] and Sheila Patterson[26] support the view that such resistance to Black workers – occasionally as an exaggerated response to the process of mental projection – can be overcome where employers take a firm stand and the trade unions give a lead.

BUSINESS ENTERPRISES

There is not much in the literature about ethnic minority businesses although within the last two years a number of small studies have been undertaken. A recent study by Muhammed Anwar of Pakistanis in Britain does illustrate a number of the basic problems. He says that one way of avoiding the difficulties and discrimination which Pakistanis faced was through becoming self-employed. For many, however, it was also the sense of prosperity, independence and respect that being self-employed brought them in their community.[27]

The study looks at 23 self-employed Pakistani men.

Table 7
Type of Businesses of the Sample

Type of Business	Number
Grocers and Butchers	06
Restaurants and Cafes	02
Personal Services	03
General Services	02
Manufacturers	03
Market Stall Traders	06
Electrical and Radio	01
Total	23

Other shopkeepers had started up business in partnership for several reasons. Among these were lack of initial capital; lack of confidence; the inability to speak English fluently and hence the need for a partner who could overcome the language barrier; someone to hold on while the other visited wholesalers or carried out deliveries; and a variety of kinship or friendship ties.[28]

What was even more important was the source of finance. Of the 23 self-employed, 22 had used their own savings and 16 had used finance from friends and relatives and six from personal business contacts. Two had finance from a Pakistani Bank and two from English Banks; but in the case of the bank finance this had come after the businesses were established and was being used for expansion.[29]

It is evident that the bulk of finance was raised through informal and personal sources as against the traditional institutional means. Allen in another study of Bradford where there were 29 respondents, 21 mentioned own savings and 21 mentioned friends and relatives as one source of finance.[30]

In both these studies the respondents were in Britain for more than five years before attempting to start up in business yet the most frequent way of raising capital was through informal and personal sources. From other studies and the experiences and contacts of community workers with an even larger number of Black businessmen, few have found capital from the traditional banking sources.

30

*"The validity of being black and saying so lies within a man's own
experience and awareness and nowhere else"*

Leslie Scafe –
Luton Harmony 1973

Chapter 3

The Educational Needs of Britain's
Black Communities

THE NUMBERS GAME

Julia McNeal has argued that the bogey of the education of
immigrant children in British schools is not so much a matter of
racial discrimination, but of concentration.[1] But one accepts her
argument only partly; for although she correctly points out that it
was not because large numbers of Black children have led to less
favourable treatment that it was condemned, but because of the fear
that "foreign enclaves" might themselves be developed within
British culture and society. She nevertheless fails to examine the
basis of that fear. It was really because these foreign enclaves were of
subject peoples whose cultures British society had not yet grown
accustomed to treating on par with Western European cultures. So
while most of the discussion was about numbers, the underlying
pressures were really about the preservation of white racial
dominance.

At a time when Blacks constituted 2.1 per cent of the total
population of the country, their children constituted some 3.3 per
cent of the total school population[2] based on the Government's
definition of an "immigrant" child for the purpose of the
Department of Education and Science statistical records. Townsend
and Britton suggest a broader definition of "immigrant" and as a
consequence arrived at the conclusion that immigrant pupils
probably constituted as much as 4.5 per cent of the school
population. While this figure would not be great in itself, it does
present a situation in which the representation of Black children as a
percentage of the total school population is twice as great as the
percentage of Blacks in the population as a whole.[3]

During the 60s and early 70s when immigrant parents were
bringing in their dependent children and while the younger than

average immigrant population was still of child-bearing age, a situation developed where the numbers of Black children as a percentage of the total school population was twice as great as the percentage of Blacks in the population as a whole. This is due to increase slightly to about two and a half times by the late 80s and then taper off slowly. What is important is that for the forseeable future there will be in British schools a larger percentage of Black children than the percentage of Blacks in the population as a whole.

Because of the settlement position, created by a complex of job opportunity, housing availability and kinship pressures, the resulting distribution of Black children has been very uneven throughout the 'country; across schools within particular conurbations and regions and even districts/boroughs, as well as across classes in particular schools. Since the basic school organisation remains the neighbourhood school, it follows that if you can influence where people do or do not live you can determine the school they attend, and hence by switching resources, human as well as material, you can determine the quality of that education. Indeed because the catchment areas of schools are arbitrary political decisions, these are open to a fair degree of gerrymandering.

We need to examine how Government sought to deal with this unevenness. By 1963 some schools in those areas of high immigrant concentration were already having percentages of Black pupils well over 30 per cent in the school system as a whole, but with some classes in the same schools having over 75 per cent of Black pupils. One such area was Southall.

While educational purists will tell you that the purpose of education is the fullest development of all the talents of the individual and the pursuit of knowledge; the politician and his educational bureaucrats use education as a means of preserving and advancing the spheres of the dominant group and its culture – Tory MP Edward Boyle, then Education Minister was one such politician.

Following a meeting with white Southall parents protesting over the number of Asian children in two Southall schools, he immediately announced in Parliament that no school should contain more than 30 per cent immigrants and pledged his support for those local authorities that tried to disperse their Black pupils throughout their schools. He offered no academic explanation on educational grounds for his decision; nor did he advance any reasons for the choice of 30 per cent over and above any other

32

percentage.

But before one feels that that decision was a peculiar Conservative approach, it is necessary to point out that the succeeding Labour Government immediately invited local authorities with "multi-racial schools" to put in requests to employ above quota staff. The unspoken argument being that 30 white children (average class size) were easier to teach than 30 children some of whom were Black. Some local authorities unashamedly made a bee line for this honeypot using every possible permutation of the numbers game. The Boyle limit of 30 per cent was slightly advanced to 33⅓ per cent by the Labour Minister's Circular 7/65. It put forward the theory, and again without evidence, that as the proportion of immigrant children in a school or class increases, the problems – again unidentified – will become more difficult to solve. Then follows the key phrase which underlined the Minister's and his Government's objective – "the chances of assimilation were remote . . ."

With a degree of mathematical certainty, the circular continued: "up to a fifth of immigrant children in any one group fit in with reasonable ease, but if the proportion goes over about one third in the school as a whole or in any one class, serious strains arise."[4] Evidently the strains referred to are those in relation to assimilation. With this Government support a consensus developed in certain quarters that Black children over a certain percentage meant uncontrollable problems. There was a certain threshold of tolerance beyond which neither class nor school could pass without direct consequences.

Despite the work of Mobey[5] and others carried out by the Centre for Environmental Studies which clearly showed that there was no evidence to justify – on the ground of academic attainment – the limiting of the Black intake into a school either by bussing, controlled entry or any other form of social engineering, the view still persisted. Indeed as long as that view held credence, administrators, teachers and racists alike all had excuses for the poor performance within the education system.

Administrators far from dispersing, engineered schools and classes above the accepted limit in order to justify their claims for additional resources for their 'problem' areas; teachers could invoke the unmanageable stresses which made teaching impossible, and the racists had a ready scapegoat for the poor performance, real or imagined, of white children.

A few local authorities did attempt the "dispersal" formula by bussing Black children who should normally have been attending inner-city schools to suburban ones. Two problems had to be faced. The Race Relations Board ruled that under the 1968 Race Relations Act, bussing was illegal if carried out for any reason other than strictly educational ones. Indeed three local authorities were investigated by the Board. Secondly, having created the myth that Black children brought with them uncontrollable stresses, white parents were reluctant to see these children transported from inner-city schools to theirs. By and large these middle class, articulate and politically sophisticated parents won that battle in round one. Dispersal never took off.

Thus, despite advice and exhortation the uneven distribution of Black pupils continued, so that by 1973 Little reported that ethnic minority children constituted 25 per cent of the total enrolment in schools in two local education authorities, 20-25 per cent in five and 15-20 per cent in a further six. That is to say, some 13 education authorities had a Black pupil population in excess of 15 per cent of their school population. He also pointed out that in 1,000 out of the 33,000 schools, ethnic minority pupils constituted over 25 per cent of those enrolled.[6]

The balloon on the numbers game nearly went up when Mrs Margaret Thatcher, Secretary of State of Education and Science, told Parliament in June 1973 that her department did not use the statistics which were then being collected annually and that they did not form the basis of any grant from her department. "None of our grant formulae are on the basis of immigrants", she said. Her statement was correct only in so far as the grants did not come from the Department of Education and Science but from the Home Office which had responsibility both for immigration control and the Government's policy of assimilating Blacks. No recent figures are available since the Form 7(1) was discontinued after that. It had until then been a supplement to the customary annual returns of all pupils.

SOCIO-ECONOMIC BACKGROUND
It is however important to note that even in 1971, 70 per cent of the Black community were concentrated in 10 per cent of the enumeration districts and here they constituted close on 20 per cent of the population. These same areas are the ones which are identified by urban decay characterised by physical and social disintegration. They represent much of the inner-city syndrome of broken homes, one-parent families, social stress and criminality.

34

School buildings are of the older type with few amenities and where teaching staff tend to be living outside of the community and subject to rapid turnover except mostly for those too old and those too incompetent to move on. This is not to deny that there are exceptionally good and competent teachers who remain to teach in these conditions out of social commitment.

For those trapped in this situation there is little natural stimulation in the environment and where, as we have shown, both parents are at work and oftimes on different shifts, inadequate mothering and parental attention is the consequence. There is general support for the conclusion drawn by Dr Pollack that insofar as West Indian children are concerned that this contributes a major part of their failure to keep pace with their white counterparts in Gesell tests of personal-social adaptive behaviour and language development.

In her study of three-year-olds in Brixton she found that a high proportion of them were non-verbal or deaf or showed signs of autistic behaviour. She predicted educational difficulties for them in the future in maintaining progress at school. She blamed inadequacy of the mothering and parental attention given to the children as the major contribution to their plight.[7]

Cross argues that the available evidence on academic achievement of ethnic minority pupils in British schools tends to suggest a connection between their low performance and the pre-school provision and the degree of stimulation ethnic minority parents give to their children.[8]

Cross looks at the results of Pollack and others and notes the development of a generalization beyond the limits of Pollack's investigations in London. He concludes that the results were "in part a reflection of the socio-economic background of ethnic minority parents which restricts the extent to which they can provide such materials required by young children (toys) and of their heavy commitment to working long hours . . . . their being unable to afford sufficient time for children." But while rejecting the results as signifying a "simple casual role" in the deprivation of Blacks in the pre-school years, he concedes that the disadvantages of the pre-school years do carry over into school experience.[9]

Many Black parents accustomed to out-of-door life and natural elements of play have been slow to respond to the heavily commercialised toy industry and life in the bedsitter or flat in a country where during winter months a lot of activity must be carried on indoors. Added to this, the shift to a society where the support of the extended families has been partially or totally removed has meant for many that the normal socialisation and educational processes of pre-school have been severely impaired.

The leader of the Inner London Education Authority expressed the difficulties faced by inner city schools in these terms:

"Schools progressively deprived of their teachable and tractable children from stable home backgrounds have had to retain an increasing population of pupils from broken homes, one-parent families and other undesirable social conditions. To them have to be added succeeding waves of immigrants, each with their own complex of problems."[10]

Bearing in mind the arguments put forward by Cross and others that there is a connection between low educational performance and preschool provision and the degree of stimulation ethnic minority children receive from their parents, and while conscious of the part parents themselves have played in this deficiency, one would be blind not to see that had it not been for the socio-economic trap in which the majority of them found themselves as a result of racial discrimination, the opportunities which they sought for their children would have been considerably enhanced.

THE LANGUAGE ISSUE

West Indian and Asian children have only been a significant factor in the modern British school population since the 1950s. Since then these numbers have grown rapidly and the growth has been unevenly spread over certain schools, mainly in older residential areas of the country's main industrial concentrations. Geoffrey Driver points out that up until 1955 most teachers in British schools taught children whose mother-tongue was English. However, since 1955 an increasing number of teachers have found growing numbers of children whose mother-tongue is Urdu or Punjabi, or who spoke an unfamiliar English dialect which they had difficulty in understanding. The problem appeared dramatic to those involved, but it was a localized phenomenon and so evoked no major national policy directives for a long time. Such local working groups as were formed of concerned teachers and local authority inspectors were involved in helping the "immigrant" pupils catch up in the use of spoken and written English.[11]

Little argues that it was not difficult for the educational system to identify and respond to the more obvious needs of the Asian pupils. It was easy to see that non-English speaking children needed additional help with the English language and it was consequently relatively simple to create the political climate within which help could be given. The same was not true for the West Indians. Their needs were more difficult to identify, subtler in nature and more threatening to the white dominant culture.[12]

West Indian and Asian children started off with two separate language problems in the early 1960s. The majority of West Indian children came from homes where English was spoken. But the form of this English varied considerably from island to island and with the educational experience of the family. Where the island was previously French or Spanish there was a carry-over of the French or Spanish idiom and in some cases a well developed form of patois has survived. In the largest of the British islands, Jamaica, Creole emerged as a well-structured English dialect and was the mode of communication for the local people. At the same time, those who had gained the advantage of secondary education, with its classical roots in Latin and Greek, spoke a form of formal English embroidered in a flowery prose. There was also a wide variation in the literacy level of the various islands and in consequence of the immigrants themselves.

On the other hand the Asian children came from homes where little or no English was spoken. The mother tongue of Urdu, Punjabi, Hindi or Gujerati being the method of communication in the home. The adult males of the family generally learned enough English to survive at work and with the aid of the more educated in the community conduct official business.

There was general agreement on the needs of Asian children as well as the methods to be used. It was a case of teaching English to a non-English speaker. Both the political will and the technical expertise were present and local education authorities and school teachers were able to respond in concert to this situation. The parents too understood the need and supported what was going on. In the case of West Indian children, it was some time before the parents themselves accepted that there was a language problem to be faced. The author was himself booed and heckled by an audience of West Indian parents in 1963 when he dared to suggest that if West Indian children were not to fall behind in English schools more attention would have to be paid to their language needs not because they did not speak English, but precisely because the English they spoke was generally of a different idiom from that used by the teachers.

Since neither parents nor teachers were identifying the problems the situation went without any attempts at remedial treatment for

37

years, while West Indian performance in schools slipped even further. It was not until 1967 that any serious attempt was made to do anything about West Indian needs in the use of the English idiom, pronunciation and intonation and in generally coming to terms with Creole interference. When we consider that the recent influx of West Indians had been well on the way in 1954, almost fifteen years had passed before a major problem affecting their well-being and future was tackled.

Townsend and Brittan, in their research study into the responses to the presence of Black and brown children in British schools, had this to say:

"It is apparent that the teaching of English to non-English speaking pupils is seen by multi-racial schools as their major task. Schools deal with this task in many different ways according to their own philosophy and to the resources made available by local education authorities. What is not clear is the level of proficiency in English at which schools decide that no further special arrangements are necessary. The question of "second stage" English following the initial achievement of literacy appears as yet to be imperfectly understood in either the need or the approach. Equally misunderstood perhaps are the need for, and the approach to, teaching pupils of West Indian origin to use the English idiom, pronunciation and intonation."[13]

The various administrative arrangements employed by local educational authorities have ranged from language centres, sometimes called induction centres, to the use of peripatetic language teachers. There remains a shortage of teachers of English as a second language, despite the additional and direct financial support received from Central Government under Section 11 of the Local Government Act 1966 which provides 75 per cent exchequer finance for certain category of staff, in which teachers of English as a second language fall.

Cross recalls that initially it had been thought that the West Indian and Asian children could "pick up the language" from their English class mates in schools. Soon, however, it became clear that there was a need for a more structured approach to their language needs. There were few skilled practitioners in their area as indeed there was a shortage of teaching material. The Schools Council supported a project in Leeds under June Derrick which produced materials for people with inadequate English. The project was also concerned with the development of course syllabii for children in junior schools. In 1967, a similar project was launched at

Birmingham University under Professors Taylor and Sinclair, to produce material for improving the language proficiency of West Indian children.[14]

Although agreeing that not all West Indian children's language problems could be attributed to Creole interference, the Birmingham project team found that Creole dialect caused interference in all areas of communication.[15]

ACHIEVEMENT and UNDERACHIEVEMENT

Cross concludes that the language needs of ethnic minority pupils have a direct link with their achievement patterns within schools as well as the question of their representation in Educational Sub-normal (ESN) schools.[16] Bernard Coard, in his book *How the Immigrant Child is made Educationally Subnormal*, explored the role of racial discrimination in the process of deciding who goes to ESN schools.[17]

The preponderance of published results support the underachievement of ethnic minority children in schools. Townsend and Brittan found that many head teachers expressed concern over the low performance of ethnic minority children as compared with their white counterparts and that they tended to be more concerned for West Indians than for Asian and Cypriot pupils.

Indeed this is no more than the author had said to his West Indian audience in 1963. What is disturbing is that few administrators recognised the relationship between this low-performance occasioned by language blockages and behavioural difficulties, and more significantly Varlaan's conclusion that where the two were found together it was more likely that the low performance consequent upon the language difficulty preceded the behavioural problems. Hence a number of West Indian children have been penalised for behavioural problems which have their genesis in the failure of the school to identify and deal with their language deficiency.

The disproportionate number of West Indian children found in schools for the educational sub-normal has never been adequately explained on educational grounds. Coard offers an analysis which lays a substantial part of the blame on racial discrimination. This is not because teachers are rabid racists; but more because they operate in a system that has permitted false assumptions of Blacks to persist. This has led to the use of a value system in relation to Blacks in general and West Indians in particular which over-rides the legitimate educational needs of the children.

The Inner London Education Authority (ILEA) conducted a series of studies the findings of which are reported by Little,[18] Barnes[19] and others. The main findings are summarised below:

(a) *At the end of primary schooling the children of New Commonwealth immigrants in the ILEA area had a reading age of approximately one year below the national norms for their age group.*

(b) *At transfer to secondary schools the ILEA bands pupils into three broad groups on verbal reasoning, English and mathematics. In each of three years, 1966, 1968 and 1971, the percentage of immigrant children fully educated in the UK, in the top band was roughly half of what should be expected and that which the indigenous pupils achieved.*

(c) *Children from different ethnic backgrounds who had been fully educated in the UK appeared to be functioning at different levels. Asians appeared to be doing as well as the indigenous population.*

(d) *There was evidence to suggest that gap in performance was widening with school career.*

(e) *West Indian children were not only functioning at a level below the indigenous population, but also below the socially disadvantaged sections of it.*

(f) *The gap between West Indian pupils and socially disadvantaged whites was demonstrable early in pupil's school career.*

(g) *The teaching profession was concerned not only with the education performance of West Indian children, but also with their behaviour in school.*

On this latter finding, Rutter, M.L. et al, in a South London study found that West Indian children showed rather more behavioural difficulties at school, but they did not differ from other children in terms of disorder shown at home. Nor did they differ in terms of emotional disturbance in any setting".[20]

Varlaan provides a link between school performance and behaviour in a study in which the relationship between reading standards and maladjusted behaviour is examined. The conclusions arrived at through this study already referred to are that "when the two conditions (reading retardation and behaviour disorder) are found together, there is a better chance that reading retardation preceded behaviour difficulties than the other way round, and second, that such a chance is positively strong when the children involved come from large families or have a West Indian background."[21] This would tend to suggest that it is the educational underachieving which is producing the maladjusted behaviour the schools often report.

The achievement of Asian pupils cited in the ILEA study has been supported by a study in Newcastle by J.H. Taylor, which showed that Asian pupils attained higher performance scores than their white counterparts.[22] So too is the underachievement of West Indian children in a study by Jennie Williams for the Dudley Council for Community Relations. She concluded that West Indian children were doing less well than their white counterparts.[23] The Redbridge study of some 600 children in junior school confirmed the underachievement of West Indian children in basic literacy and numeracy skills.[24]

The conventional wisdom is that having taught Asian children sufficient English to give them fluency in communication, they proceed to do as well as their English counterparts. On the other hand researcher after researcher measures and measures once again the underachievement of West Indian children as though the process of recording their failure was some sort of academic fetish. Either West Indian children fail because of the inherent nature of 'Black' children's underachievement as Jensen and Eysenck would have us believe or there are factors contributory to their failure that can and must be overcome.

The author's own teaching experience in the West Indies and the United Kingdom leads him to affirm most unequivocally that West Indian children are in no way less teachable than white English children and can be expected to perform as well as, given the correct stimulus. But the correct stimulus cannot be generated by an expectancy of failure. Indeed so much of the literature is of West Indian failure, that the Commission for Racial Equality took almost a year to decide to publish the results of a study by Driver into the recorded examination results of 2,300 school leavers in five multi-racial secondary schools outside the inner city environment which showed that in those five schools West Indian boys and girls were, for the most part, doing better than their white counterparts. Even then they could not bring themselves to endorse the results.

Driver had consistently made it plain that he was not seeking to draw any generalisations from the study. It was a study of five schools outside the inner city environment. The study was financially supported by the Commission for Racial Equality, who, having taken some time to decide on publication, eventually did so with a diplomatic distancing from the results. The five major results were these:[25]

1. West Indian girls and boys achieved results that were for the most part, better than those obtained by English boys and girls.

2. West Indian boys and girls have in some cases tended to overtake English class-mates in the course of their secondary schools careers.

3. Among English pupils, the boys usually have better results at 16-plus than the girls. By contrast, West Indian girls do better than West Indian boys.

4. Comparing the results for English and West Indian pupils – English language, maths and science – it was found that it was usually the English boys and girls who got the poorest average results for these critical subjects.

5. Asian pupils got higher average results than either the English or West Indian pupils except in English language.

Driver argues that "the most important finding of his study is the contrapuntal trend in the performance of English boys and girls and West Indian boys and girls",[26] but others may feel that it is the first step in dismantling the inflammatory and misleading theories of Arthur Jensen and H.J. Eysenck about the inherent nature of "Black" children's underachievement. It also challenges the concept of the "cumulative deficit" in education which appeared to have been established by the ILEA study.

Extracts of the study were published in *New Society,* a quality, middle-of-the-road weekly that prides itself on its liberal academic tradition, in mid-January 1980. Its correspondents' column was still publishing letters six weeks later – the vast majority condemning the research as spurious and likely to lead to complacency at a time when everybody knew that West Indian children were doing badly and posed the greatest challenge to English schools.

What the Commission for Racial Equality and many of the correspondents failed to grasp was the fact that there are certain conditions under which West Indian children can and will do well; and the fact that many of them are doing less well is not to say, that all of them are underachieving. But such was the conventional wisdom that Driver's limited statement of success, although consistent with what is known to exist in several schools in the country, was unable to find ready acceptance.

While Cross argues that there might well be "different factors in the background socialization of ethnic minority pupils as against that of indigenous pupils which place them at a disadvantage in the education system.[27] Driver contends that his study reveals that "in terms of the ethnic qualities, these boys and girls demonstrate positive qualities which dominate their performance and overshadow the influence of the system of schooling as a whole. Such positive qualities and the strength of the cultural patterns which create them, are well recognised in the case of Asian children, but less so where West Indians are concerned".[28]

Assessing the response to Driver, the author concludes that what white society most resented was the suggestion which Driver advanced that there were certain positive ethnic qualities, created by the cultural patterns of the ethnic minorities which dominated their performance at school and which overshadowed the influence of the system of schooling as a whole. He was in this respect threatening not only their cultural dominance but also their latent feelings of racial superiority.

TEACHER ATTITUDES and TRAINING

There is agreement on the importance of teacher attitudes and expectations in developing the favourable climate for a child's learning processes. The literature is full of examples of negative attitudes, bordering on subliminal racism, held by teachers.

Perhaps the attitudes of teachers is best summed up in the contribution of Sam Fisher and others at the conference convened by the Secretary of State for Education and Science in April 1975, on "Educational Disadvantages: Perspectives and Policies", when he said that the National Union of Teachers (NUT) was certainly not against Blacks, and recognised that minority groups did have special needs, he agreed that those needs should be dealt with. However, he added, the NUT were against the identification in the public mind of ethnic minorities with problems. Being Black was not in itself an educational disadvantage. A substantial number of his sixth formers were from minority groups and they contributed greatly to his school's athletic, drama and music.[29] He was not even conscious of how deeply he had fallen into the stereotyping process of Blacks as good performers and entertainers. It would have been a far different statement if he had been able to say that they contributed greatly to all facets of the school's life.

Miss Elsie Clayton, the President of the NUT, added her voice to the cry by saying –

"It is a disgrace that the Educational Disadvantage Unit should have been set up only in response to a report of the Select Committee on Race Relations and Immigration. Immigrants were only one element in the realm of disadvantage and should not be emphasised in case this might provoke white resentment".

She was supported by Mr Fred Jarvis, NUT General Secretary, who argued that it was important that the concern with immigrants should not be overstressed, since they represented only a minority of the disadvantaged. The idea that that conference and the various other initiatives had come about as the result of a response to the Select Committee on Race Relations and Immigration had set the discussion off on the wrong footing.[30]

They were completely unable to see that while it was possible for Blacks to suffer from the normal socio-economic problems like the rest of society, they also carried the added problems of cultural dislocation and the effects of racial prejudice and discrimination.

But the story does not end there. These negative attitudes are taken into the classroom as well as the staff room. In the classroom they have a demoralising effect upon Black pupils especially when conveyed by non-verbal communication or through expressions which indicate a lack of respect or appreciation for the pupil's originating culture and mother tongue. In the staff room they reinforce staff prejudices against Blacks and frustrate young Black teachers in their attempts to bring a positive element into the situation by raising the generally low esteem teachers have of their Black pupils and their culture.

Driver, in his discussion on "Classroom Stress and School Achievement", looks at the difficulties posed for classroom management by the presence of pupils with distinctive physical features, gestures and other codes of communication than those of the majority society. He illustrates how these force limitation on the teacher's managerial and teaching roles and "influence their attitudes towards those individuals who seemed to be the focus of their difficulties."[31]

There is a graphic paragraph in Thomas Cottle's book, *Black Testimony,* in which a young Black teacher is relating her experiences and the pressures placed upon her by both Black and white societies. In it there is a vivid description of white teacher attitudes. The Black teacher speaking:

"And it happens with my colleagues. I hear it all the time. They defend me during September, throughout the year, but I hear the

comments they make, like; 'We have one, why do we need more? Or; 'She's different, we won't find any more as good, because she's not like them'. Or: 'Are we running an employment bureau for West Indians. Or: are we supposed to be teachers?'. Now with all this going on, do you honestly think I'm going to stand up at a meeting and propose that we should have more minority teachers and begin to have minority administrators?"[32]

But it is not only the issue of teacher attitudes and general low esteem of their Black pupils that matters; there is also the problem of training; or lack of it. Indeed, Little concludes that "teacher training institutions were slow to respond to the training implications of a multi-racial education system, it was only in the second half of the 1960s that colleges of education began to pay some attention to the needs of immigrant pupils." In support of this position he cites the Robbins Committee Report 1963, which stated that one of the aims of higher education was the transmission of a common culture and the common standards of citizenship, and argues that the Robbins Committee had only the indigenous culture and its standards in mind and "saw no need at the time to relate these to a multi-cultural society." It was the James Committee in 1971 that concluded that in any general education scheme, an understanding of the multi-cultural nature of society should be included.[33]

This was a bold statement since it was not yet universally politically accepted that we did have a multi-cultural society or that the trends towards one were irreversible. This concept of cultural pluralism was dramatically opposed to the Government's originally stated position of assimilaton. Beyond that, however, was the fact that it would take time for the teacher training institutions to respond favourably and intelligently to the multi-cultural concept, and for a variety of reasons they had shown themselves reluctant to make the necessary changes in curriculum development.

The James Committee report was reinforced in 1973 by a report by the Parliamentary Select Committee on Race Relations and Immigration which recommended that all students on teacher training, whether on initial or post-graduate courses, should be made to recognise that wherever they went to teach, they would be doing so in a multi-cultural society.[34] The Committee's recommendation was made to meet the argument put up by some teachers' colleges that the vast majority of their graduates went to teach in all white schools or schools with few Black pupils and so did not really need elaborate training in multi-cultural issues.

The Community Relations Commission published in 1974, a report *Teacher Education for a Multi-Cultural Society,*[35] recommending that all students should be given an awareness of the educational implications of a multi-racial society, that this awareness should also be included in courses for other students studying in other institutions of higher education; that special options should be available to students who plan to teach in multi-racial areas and that colleges in co-operation with local education authorities should use their expertise and facilities in organising a range of in-service courses.

Little, while admitting that there are some notable examples of colleges where the training of teachers for teaching in a multi-racial society is taken seriously, contends that they are in a minority and that "there is still little evidence that colleges of education are approaching the education of minority groups in anything more than a haphazard way."[36]

HOME/SCHOOL LIAISON

Another feature of successful schooling is the linkage between the school and the home. Cross in his study of Education Priority Areas (EPA)[37] reveals all his respondents suggested "that Home/School contact among parents of ethnic minority children was very inadequate" and that for many of his respondents this was cited as an important contribution in the under-achievement of ethnic minority children compared to their indigenous counterparts. Respondents also saw the mystique which surrounded the school in the minds of many ethnic minority parents as greatly contributing to the lack of contact and effective liaison.

The study also demonstrates the level of participation in groups like the Parent/Teacher Associations is largely among the middle-class parents and has done little or nothing to effect liaison at those levels where it was most needed. It recognised that in some cases one or the other or both of two strategies were being adopted – that of trying to involve parents in activities of the school which were not connected with their children's education, e.g. adult language classes for Asians on the school's premises; and that of appointing school liaison staff in the form of Home/School visitors.

In the middle-class dominated Parent/Teacher Associations teacher and parent meet together, discuss matters of common interest and can be seen to be joined in the common pursuit of the pupil's development. For many Black parents the fear of the imposing image which the school presents both physically and

46

psychologically, the unwelcoming attitude of teachers to parents whose work schedules do not allow the flexibility to attend on their demand and the inability of many parents to cope with the language in which the whole school dialogue is conducted, combine to make it impossible for the normal channels of contact between home and school to remain open.

BLACK STUDIES

But the distance between Black pupil and school is even greater. There are many large comprehensive schools with 20 per cent and more of whose pupils are Black, and whose corridors extend for over a mile. On their walls pictures are hung and at convenient recesses pieces of sculpture and other works of art are placed. Yet none of this depicts any other art form than that of western European culture. The whole visual impact of the message to the Black child is that he is not part of the school. What it says to the white child is that the Black child is an alien intruder into his world.

The course content reinforces, without directly saying so, the superiority of white society. The heroes are white, the doers of great exploits are white, there are no models of Black excellence to which the Black child can look with self-pride and dignity. To achieve an equal society, a positive effort at teaching equality must begin with developing mutual respect in the cultural achievements and contribution to world thought and development.

It is part of the conventional wisdom that ethnic minority children would respond more favourably to the education system if the curriculum of the school and its environment were made more responsive to their cultural backgrounds. It is felt that this would reduce the alienation between these children and the school and thus improve their performance at school. Coard, Little, Morris, Cross and Barrow to mention a few, all accept this position; but what is less universally accepted is the manner in which this ought to be achieved.

Prince Charles, in a speech to the Anthropological Institute, said that an acquaintance with anthropology could enable those who never had a chance to leave this island, see other countries and witness the lives of their inhabitants, to understand something of the problems and difficulties experienced by immigrant communities in Great Britain. He added: "The more it is possible for this sort of enlightenment to spread the more likely are we to reach a level of civilized tolerance in a multi-racial society."[38]

Sam Morris, a pioneer in the concept of Black Studies in Britain, argued that it is important for the black elements in British society to have what he called an *aide memoire* of their existence and contribution to the society, some appreciation of their distinctive heritage which they have added to the total social existence.[39] Indeed it was to his credit that Radio London ran a twenty programme series in the Autumn 1972/Spring 1973.

Even some of those who were in favour of the idea could not accept the term "Black Studies" and sought to have the title changed to "Ethnic Studies", others rejected it outright on the grounds that it was divisive as though the need for it had not been brought about by a divisive society.[40]

Cross quotes two respondents in his study as saying this.[41] One : "I am against Black Studies. If you select one aspect of the curriculum like that you set up a reaction among white kids. I believe in a balanced curriculum using an indirect approach to race relations. You'll get a socially just society if you provide all children with sufficient educational resources". The other: "Learning the cultural background of your family is important but this is not the job of the school, it is the responsibility of the home."

Leslie Scafe, the editor of Luton Harmony, wrote this in 1973:–
"Some of the objections to Black Studies are motivated by fear. It is assumed that if the Black person learned too much about his history, he will become angry and this will increase social conflict in society. It is, however, the lack of full knowledge that is dangerous. A man can only be fully liberated through a knowledge of the truth. Yet again, there are others who give the impression that they are put off the term "Black Studies" because the word "Black" has been given associations of ugliness and evil. They avert their eyes and try to stop their ears. So they want us to have "ethnic" studies or they say "your face is not black, it is brown . . ." The validity of being black and saying so lies within a man's own experience and awareness and nowhere else."[42]

Morris sums up the position this way:–
"The purpose of Black Studies in Britain is not to secure a panacea for all the ills of Black people, it is not to find a substitute for other studies, it is not to secure academic distinction and it is not an end in itself. It's purpose is to help the Black person to regain his lost identity and to help him understand his position in the world today. It is to encourage him to qualify for living and thriving in the industrial competitive complex which is Britain and Europe today."[43]

Agreeing with the sentiments of Prince Charles, Morris makes the point that Black Studies, though of particular relevance to the Black child should be pursued by all.

But the prime example of the cultural worth of ethnic minorities in British schools came from the following statement of one administrator within a local education authority:–

"Mother-tongue instruction is a problem for the community, not for the school. We have had requests for Gujarati and Urdu to be taught in schools but we are against it. If they live and work here, their first need is to speak and write English. If we taught mother-tongue in schools, we would have thirty or forty languages in some schools. If ethnic minorities want their language taught at weekends, that's fine."[44]

The same local education authority freely offers French, German, Spanish, Latin, Greek and Russian in its schools. In fact, it makes quite a virtue out of bilingualism. The problem arises when the second language is that of a Black ethnic minority culture. The sad fact is the low esteem in which Black culture is held and difficulty in convincing education authorities that Black cultures may be different, but that does not make them inferior.

The author cannot accept the position of those teachers who argue that the learning of the cultural background of other groups in society is not a matter for the school. He takes the view put forward by Sam Morris that the introduction of Black Studies in schools is not something for Blacks alone but for all pupils. It is not the introduction of a separate subject but the integration of multi-cultural thought to all areas of the school curriculum, thus giving Black pupils a place and an identity in the body of social life.

YOUTH SERVICE and the NEEDS of ADOLESCENTS

The Youth Service is viewed as an appendage of the education service and is locally the responsibility of the local education authority and nationally of the Department of Education and Science. As far back as 1967, the Hunt Committee in reporting on immigrants and the youth service said: "If England is not to be the scene of race riots then the time for action is now. Tomorrow may be too late."[45] One difficulty in adequately dealing with the problem of Black youth springs from the concept that the youth service is no more than the Cinderella of the Education Service and that white youth are equally disadvantaged by it. In this respect the view of Tony Ottey cited by Cross is significant:–

"It may be that Blacks are on the same boat as poor whites; we are on different decks."[46]

49

Local authorities are required by statute to provide for the needs of young people between the ages of 14-20 in partnership with voluntary agencies. It is this complex that we must examine. Sir John Maud in setting out the objectives of the Youth Service defined them as:

"To offer individual young people in their leisure time opportunities of various kinds, complementary to those of home, formal education and work, to discover and develop their personal resources of body, mind and spirit and thus the better to equip themselves to live the lives of mature, creative and responsible members of a free society."[47]

Indeed, local authorities and the voluntary agencies have interpreted these objectives in their own way and consistent with their own philosophical orientation. The youth service information centre (now the National Youth Bureau) in a survey of local authorities and voluntary agencies met with so disappointing a response for information, especially from the areas of high Black concentration, that they were moved to question whether those responsible were so inundated with requests that they could no longer find time and patience to reply or whether they considered the area of race and the provision for young immigrants such a hot potato as not to submit accounts or yet whether there was really nothing to report.[48]

The Community Relations Commission, in its study in 1977, found that although some 33 per cent of Black adolescents had used youth club facilities at some time, only 10 per cent were still attending; Asians were found to be less likely to use the facilities than either West Indian or Cypriot youth; and that the Hunt Committee's recommendations were being interpreted so narrowly and rigidly that many agencies were distinctly uneasy about providing uni-racial facilities.[49]

At subsequent seminars conducted by the CRC for youth workers and youth service policy makers, it became clear that policy makers found themselves operating within considerable financial and staffing constraints and that there was a sense of low morale and isolation among youth workers confronted with Black youths facing problems of racial discrimination, cultural identity, homelessness, unemployment and conflict with the law.

It was not difficult to reach the conclusion that the youth service as it existed was not relevant to many of the problems of young Blacks in multi-racial areas, and was never intended to be. Indeed, in a foreword to the report of these seminars Lord Hunt said:

50

"The hopes and fears we entertained ten years ago appear to be as valid today as they were then, although the ratio of one to the other may have changed. The message remains the same: The need for a positive policy in regard to community relations in all their aspects; a readiness by everyone concerned to face up to the problems; the will to overcome them; and the means to provide the essential resources. The matter of resolve is crucial, for without it, the evils of racism will gain ground."[50]

Interviews conducted by the CRC have shown, and the author's experience in Wolverhampton has confirmed, that Black youth were seldom able to make full use of the conventional youth service because of the hostility of young whites and the fear of rejection, and that white youths tended to leave where the worker insisted on admitting Blacks. It required a tremendous amount of effort and courage to maintain a multiracial club. John Eggleston in his study has found that the only areas where Black involvement in youth facilities has improved are those in which multiracial provision exists.[51]

Margaret Bone, in her study of the youth service, offers three reasons for the relative low participation of ethnic minority young people in the youth service.[52] Firstly, there is the nature of the immigrant communities themselves and their cultural norms of control over their children. Secondly, the pattern of social selection which appears to be associated with a strong attachment to youth clubs if applied to Blacks would produce a lower participation, and thirdly, there is the changing demographic characteristic of the community.

Despite the Hunt Committee warning in 1967 that if Britain was to avoid race riots, immediate action needed to be taken in respect of the needs of Black youth, little has happened. Agencies have been distinctly unhappy about providing facilities to be used by one racial group. Hence the needs of Asians and Cypriots in general and their girls in particular have, by and large, gone unanswered.

Little training has been given to youth workers who have the task of dealing with young Blacks facing all sorts of problems of racial discrimination, loneliness, unemployment, cultural identity and conflict with the law. Having failed to deal with the issue of multiracialism in the schools, it is impossible to expect the less qualified, more inadequately staffed and less effectively resourced youth clubs to cope with teenage problems at their most sensitive and acute.

Black youth in multi-racial areas have found the traditional youth club an irrelevance in so far as their needs are concerned. What is

51

more, where they have attempted to use the facilities they have found that white members leave the club, allowing it to become predominantly Black. Youth leaders unable to cope with their new clientele soon lose control of the club and the local education authority has moved in and closed the facility.

SELF-HELP

A reaction to the lack of provision to meet their needs by the normal institutions in society have given rise to a number of projects designed and run by the community. These include a number of educational schemes, ranging from head-start to supplementary classes. The process is still young and has so far been funded by Urban Aid, the Commission for Racial Equality and a small number of Trusts. No systematic assessments of the projects have so far been undertaken, but project developers seem pleased with the progress to date and both parents and teachers attest to the help children have received from these schemes.

The Commission for Racial Equality in a document published in 1980, says that the supportive ethnic framework of self-help projects has been a major factor in the restoration of a sense of identity and self-confidence among young disadvantaged Blacks. The development of the self-help movement has involved and mobilised local Black communities in a way which could not have been expected from statutory provision.[53]

These schemes designed by the community, for the community and run by the community have demonstrated dramatically how wide the gap between community need and service delivery really is. They have also shown that the needs of the community can be met and without the high level of resource allocation which is always claimed to be the restraining factor.

They have illustrated that if the normal institutions of society were sympathetic and responsive, they, with their much more sophisticated management and service delivery techniques, could have aptly coped with Black needs. While it is true to say that the self-help movement has mobilised local Black communities, and developed a new socially aware Black leadership in a way that could not have been expected from the statutory bodies, it must still be the objective that Black needs will be met substantially by the traditional statutory agencies.

If this day is to be hastened, one must see a strengthening of the self-help movement to a point where it is able to negotiate on its own behalf with both Central and Local Government. At the present, the funding of self-help schemes through the Self-Help Fund of the Commission for Racial Equality, local authority and Central Government, through Urban Aid and Inner City funds and a variety of smaller trusts gives rise to project-oriented funding rather than responsive resource allocation based on strategic policy planning.

A SECOND CHANCE

After the youth service, it is the post-school educational institutions run by local authorities and referred to as the Further Education system, to distinguish them from the Higher Education system of polytechnics and universities, that suffer from the effects of cut backs and recession. These are important in that for many young people they represent a second chance for those who missed out on the first time round at regular schooling.

But like so much of British education, they were slow to respond to the changing demands of the community which they served and to recognise or accept the trend towards multi-racialism. Even when they had large numbers of Black youth virtually knocking on their door, they could not make links with the new communities.

It was clear from the basic problems of immigrants and their settlement that new pressures would be put on the post-school education institutions as they attempted to face up to the demands of a multi-racial society. In 1976, the Community Relations Commission published a study on the use of the Further Education services by ethnic minority students.[54] It found use to be very patchy, even though substantial numbers were making use of the services in certain areas. The study concluded that the pattern of use could be accounted for by failure of the schools to equip these young people with educational qualifications, extensive discrimination in employment and the concentration of ethnic minorities in deprived inner city areas.

The study divided those ethnic minorities whose needs were not being met by the Further Education services into four groups: school leavers, adults at work or unemployed needing basic education, groups with special needs and potential workers in professional fields. It argued for a closer relationship between colleges and their committees and urged that not only teaching and curriculum development but also admissions, procedures, counselling provision and social arrangements all need to take account of cultural differences and special needs.

RESOURCES

A Working Party of Chief Education Officers concluded that being responsible for multi-racial schools meant making political, administrative and educational decisions about inter-group relations, allocation of resources, the possibility of positive discrimination and involvement with agencies outside the school.[55]

Little contends that there is inadequate financial aid to authorities and schools under stress.[56] In this view he concurs with the Parliamentary Select Committee, which in 1973 had this recommendation to make:–

"First, that consideration be given to the establishment of a central fund to which local education authorities could apply for resources to meet the special education needs of immigrant children and adults; second, that local education authorities should be required, as a condition of using the department's resources and services, to report regularly and fully on the situation in their area and what they are doing about it, third, that an immigrant education advisory unit should be set up in the Department of Education and Science."[57]

The Government in its response rejected all three elements of the recommendation. It took the view that where immigrants and their descendants live in the older urban and industrial areas, the majority of their children were likely to share with the indigenous children of those areas the educational disadvantages associated with an impoverished environment. The Government, therefore, believed that immigrant pupils would benefit increasingly from special help given to all those suffering from educational disadvantage.

Little contends that this position ignores the issue of newness, language and culture on the one hand and the extent to which racial discrimination creates problems to which the school must respond.[58] In this latter argument he is supported by Government White Paper on racial discrimination which acknowledged that while other groups have been disadvantaged "few other groups in society display all the accumulated disadvantages found amongst the Black communities."[59]

In rejecting the case for a central fund for the education of immigrants the Government argued that the case appeared to rest on two arguments. Firstly, the burden which fell more heavily on some local authorities than on others because of the uneven pattern of immigrant settlement and secondly that local authorities would not take initiatives to improve the education of immigrants in the absence of such a central fund. While it accepted the first of these

54

arguments and would continue to support the provision of Section 11 of the Local Government Act 1966, it could see no evidence to support the second argument. It remained Government view that if specific grants for particular aspects of education in which the local authorities had previously enjoyed discretion were to be introduced the effect might be to reduce the scope of local responsibility.[60]

Little accepts that there is weight in the argument about "local responsibility" but says that it is the particular circumstances of multi-racial areas that makes it unconvincing. The uneven distribution of Black communities concentrated on socially disadvantaged areas and the existence of racial hostility means that many areas have "neither the resources nor political will to take the necessary action to achieve general educational objectives like equality of opportunity."[61]

Commenting to the House of Commons on the failure of Urban Aid to meet the needs of Blacks in multi-racial areas, Alex Lyon, then Minister of State at the Home Office, said:–

"Over the years it (Urban Aid) has widened simply from the Black commitment to a helpful initiative on urban deprivation. I believe that it would be better if it were restricted to its original purpose."[62]

"To maintain that colour is irrelevant is to treat a moral axiom as if it were a fact: what is, can be very different from what should be."

HMSO. Council Housing Purpose,
Procedures and Priorities.

Chapter 4

The Housing Trap and the Black Experience

HOUSING CONDITIONS OF MINORITY HOUSEHOLDS

In 1977, the Department of the Environment issued a consultative document on Housing Policy. In the foreword the Secretary of the Environment wrote:–

"Nevertheless the rising housing standards of the great majority contrast sharply and starkly with those of people still living in housing lacking basic amenities, in over-crowded conditions, or have to share against their will."[1]

While one accepts the position of the Secretary of State for the Environment in his assessment that the rising housing standards of the great majority of people in society "contrasts sharply and starkly with those people still living in poor or unsuitable housing", nowhere is that assessment more true than in the case of Black Britain. All the available evidence supports the conclusion that Blacks are disproportionately represented in areas of housing stress and that they are there not out of sheer choice, but because a complex of circumstances, not the least of them being racial discrimination, have come together to create a housing trap for many of them.

The Community Roots Resource Centre, in response to the consultative document, argued that any attempts to produce a framework of policy which ameliorated that position had particular relevance and benefit to ethnic minority groups in the UK because it was the Blacks who were concentrated in those areas of housing stress about which the Government was concerned.[2]

In a national survey carried out by Political and Economic Planning (PEP), *The Facts of Racial Disadvantage*, it is shown that Blacks live in older property (88 per cent compared with 48 per cent

56

of the general population live in properties built before 1940), in property which is structurally poor (72 per cent compared with 46 per cent live in properties which are externally in poor or average condition); more likely to be living in shared households (25 per cent compared with 4 per cent); more frequently lacking in basic amenities (37 per cent of Blacks compared with 18 per cent of the general population are without exclusive use of both hot water and inside WC); and on average living in greater overcrowded conditions (on average Blacks are living at a density of 1.75 persons per bedroom, compared with 1.25 among whites).[3]

A report produced by the Department of the Environment revealed that minority groups are disproportionately located in areas of housing stress. It shows that 70 per cent of the ethnic minority population are concentrated in 10 per cent of enumeration districts. In these areas they constitute an average of just over a fifth of the local population. When these 10 per cent of enumeration districts are compared with others on indicators of housing deprivation, it is found that they contain nearly three times as many households living at a density of 1.5 persons per room, over twice as many households in privately furnished accommodation and only half as many in council housing.[4]

Table 8
Housing Tenure

	West Indians (1974 PEP)	Asians (1974 PEP)	General Population (Housing & Construction Statistics 1974)
	%	%	%
Owner Occupied	50	76	54
Rented from			
Council	26	4	29
Privately Rented	24	19	17

Source: CRC: Housing in Multi-Racial Areas. London 1976, page 9

In their report, the Working Party of Housing Directors are at pains to make the point that they disagree with the commonly held view that minority households overcrowd or live in poor conditions out of choice. They assert that their examination of the evidence shows that there are no differences between the aspirations of Black

57

and white households in so far as the quality of housing is concerned. They conclude that inadequate space standard and poor conditions are largely the results of the weak position of minority households in the housing market.[5] This was indeed a bold assertion on their part, but having made it, they failed to follow through and explore the reasons for this position being as weak as it is.

Rashmin Desai explains the high owner-occupation and low council tenancy of Asians by the strong desire on their part to own their own homes and an equally strong wish to avoid becoming council tenants.[6] Cross adds to this the fact that their households and family size predispose them to buy the larger but older Victorian type house in the inner city areas which are relatively cheap and somewhat inexpensive compared to property which was built after 1940.[7] The PEP survey of racial minorities found that owner-occupation was correlated with high concentrations of immigrants and low availability of council housing; and reflected an effort to secure appropriate accommodation for relatively larger households and families at prices they could afford.

While West Indians have made greater use of council housing than Asians, and Asians constitute a higher percentage of owner-occupiers than West Indians, they have both ended up at the bottom of the housing pile – whether public or private sector. Their efforts to find accommodation for their families at prices they could afford, convenient for getting to work, and providing reasonable choice for education of their children have not infrequently come up against both direct and indirect discrimination.

This has left them trapped for the most part in the older Victorian-type houses of the inner city areas. As has been pointed out, in the 10 per cent of enumeration districts where 70 per cent of the Blacks live, they constitute on average just over 20 per cent of the population. These districts are the very areas which contain three times the average level of overcrowding, twice as much private furnished accommodation and half the average availability of council housing.

The quality of life which Blacks experience is clearly associated with the level of access to adequate housing and there is a direct link between access and the housing policies of both central and local Government. In so far as Blacks are concerned attempts to improve the lower end of the housing market need to take account of three things: (1) the presence of special needs in multi-racial areas (2) that the mechanics of the housing system discriminates either directly or indirectly against Blacks; (3) the importance of race as a dimension or characteristic within the process of policy formation.

SPECIAL HOUSING NEEDS IN MULTI-RACIAL AREAS

Over and above the normal needs of the area, multi-racial areas do present a number of special housing needs. Depending on the composition of the Black population in the areas one is likely to find a permutation of the following special needs:– homeless West Indian teenage youth; homeless teenage Asian girls; one-parent families; ethnic elderly and multi-generation families.

As the number of West Indian youth with poor educational attainment who have become unemployed and with time alienated from society has grown, so too have they lost contact with their parents and drifted into a state of homelessness. Few local authorities have adequate provision for these young people, and in many towns community self-help groups have sprung up and tried to deal with the problems through the provision of hostels. Since 1976 Housing Departments of local authorities have been empowered to buy houses for use as hostels without having to seek prior approval from the Department of the Environment.[8] The local authority can by this means help these groups.

While these groups have been able to provide a roof over the heads of these young people, they have seldom been able to provide the level of support needed or the professional counselling necessary to effect full restoration to the state of being a dignified citizen within society. Even with some local and central Government funding the amenities provided were very much at the lower end of the market and compared unfavourably with local authority-owned and run hostels. In many cases, therefore, it can be argued that local authorities while receiving the kudos for assisting and supporting community effort, were in fact getting a service provided on the cheap, knowing it in many cases to be sub-standard, while being able to wash their hands of any failure.

Not-with-standing the above, there is evidence that hostels properly run and supervised have an important role to fulfil in helping those deprived young people in regaining their place in society. It must not be forgotten, however, that this is a primary responsibility of government and that where local groups are contributing their special knowledge of the needs of the young people this ought not to lead to a diminution in the other aspects of the service which the local authorities ought to provide.

A number of groups have developed some useful initiatives in the Black community itself. In the Handsworth area of Birmingham, the

59

Handsworth Black Community Workers offer accommodation to 15 homeless youngsters at Harambee House. A similar scheme for five young men in Wolverhampton is run by the Wolverhampton Harambee Association. Melting Pot, in the Brixton area of Lambeth, runs several houses giving accommodation for some 70 young people. The Harlesden Project in Brent offers both hostel accommodation and bed-sitting rooms for those more capable of leading their own lives and requiring less supervision. The number is growing steadily.

In the report of the Working Party of Housing Directors, some attention is paid to two areas where the housing needs of the West Indian community may differ from the indigenous population:–

"The first situation is where there is no marriage but a stable cohabitation arrangement. Housing departments and housing visitors in particular, need sensitivity and clear understanding of such family situations if they are to make the best provision for those households. Some local authorities grant tenancies in the mother's name if there is a cohabiting situation, even if this means she must take responsibility for rent payments . . . Alternatively, joint tenancies may be offered. The second group is the very young West Indian mother with no male support."[9]

In an unpublished report available from the Commission for Racial Equality, Marion Cutting describes her study at the Catholic Housing Aid Service. It revealed that it was necessary in assessing rehousing options to take into ccount the strong feelings on the part of West Indian single mothers about staying in familiar areas, the fear of discrimination in getting a new job; the problem of finding a friendly child-minder in the new area; and the worry over losing community support, all played a part in the single mother's attitude towards rehousing, according to the study.

The growing culture gap between Asian youths and their parents is particularly marked in the expectations of Asian girls fully educated in Britain. This has been reflected in ways in which the girls wish to exert their sense of independence. The ensuing conflicts have led to a number of girls becoming homeless, either because they have left home when the pressures have become too great or because of the fear of violence against them by their parents or older brothers. Some who had not rebelled while at home, have subsequently found husbands who they marry after a traditionally arranged marriage and were unwilling to accept their views of what being an Asian wife ought to be. A steadily increasing number of matrimonial conflicts has developed and with them an increase in battered wives within the Asian community. Here too the community has responded with hostel provision and other forms of sheltered accommodation. In Coventry, Wolverhampton, Leicester, Manchester, Southall and other towns and cities small community houses have been set up with the aid of the local authorities concerned.

The Finer Committee did not hide the feelings of inadequacy they had over dealing with the problems of one-parent families within the Black communities and contented themselves in expressing the fond hope that their recommendations would be equally relevant to Black Britons. Sadly, the Finer recommendations have had only sporadic implementation and have not as a rule been implemented in those local authority areas where they could have been most expected to have affected the lives of Black people.

Another special housing need is that of the elderly. On this matter Celia Pyke Lees and Sue Gardiner in their study of the ethnic elderly conclude that they represent a mere 3 per cent of the total population of ethnic minorities compared with 20 per cent of the general population.[10] Because of the demographic breakdown of immigrant communities the percentage of elderly is likely to rise in the future.

They found that although different family systems existed in the territories from which the Black immigrants came, there was broadly speaking a common attitude towards the care of the elderly. It was customary for the extended family system to contain the elderly cared for by their relatives who were seen to be responsible for them. However, they found evidence of this breaking down as ethnic minority families drifted towards the development of nuclear households. Local authority policy makers must naturally take this trend into consideration. With increasing numbers of their elderly beginning to be found in traditional residential homes and sheltered housing accommodation they will need to be prepared to cope with the problems posed by language, diet, religion and past family patterns.

David Smith and Anne Whalley, in their study, found that while large families were a minority compared to small families on local authority housing waiting lists, ethnic minority groups formed a disproportionate share of the larger families.[11]

On the other end of the spectrum, where the extended family has survived, multi-generation families may opt to live together thus creating a need for larger than usual units of housing. This may mean in some instances that the local authority will have to be prepared to offer a joint tenancy. Not all local authorities have been

61

willing to do this.

ACCESS to PUBLIC HOUSING

When looking at the mechanics of the housing system and how it discriminates directly or indirectly against the interests of Blacks in the housing market, it is necessary to look separately at the public sector as distinct from the private sector and the quasi-public section of the housing associations.

Until recently there was a three-in-five chance that, compared with their white counterparts, a West Indian or an Asian would have been unaware of the existence of council housing. David Smith concluded from survey evidence that only 56 per cent of Asians and West Indians compared with 85 per cent of the rest of the population were aware of the existence of council housing.[12] Considering this fact the Working Party of Housing Directors felt that publicity was of fundamental importance together with a more effective system of ensuring that social workers, health visitors, environmental health officers and community groups register any of their clients on waiting list in housing need.[13]

In addition, there were other barriers to an individual getting a home. There was the length of residence in the borough to contend with; then there was the question of whether or not one was British and finally whether or not one was an owner-occupier. None of these barriers bore any direct relation to housing needs per se, yet indeed each had a negative bearing on access for Black families.

The Community Roots Resource Centre, in their memorandum to the Department of Environment, made the point that although many Blacks were owner-occupiers, their homes were at the lower end of the housing market and were of such condition as would make them eligible for council housing on the criteria of housing need. Any exclusion solely on the grounds of owner-occupation was an unhelpful bind.[14]

Experience has shown that some authorities will not register single men needing family accommodation pending the arrival of their families and that homeless individuals, whatever the reason for their homelessness, can be expected to be housed in the poorest and least desirable accommodation.

The more recent speed up of access to council housing can be explained partly because most minority communities have now been here in Britain long enough to satisfy even the most stringent qualification and partly because the 1976 Race Relations Act made exclusion on grounds of nationality illegal.

The Cullingworth Report and its recommendations on residence qualifications are worth mentioning here, not because they refer specifically to Blacks, but more so because they established the strength of the debate on access to council housing in relation to Blacks. The major recommendation is:–

"Conditions differ so greatly between access that absolute uniformity is not possible. Nonetheless, we are firmly of the conviction that these should be no barrier to acceptance on a housing list. We regard this of importance both in relation to the rights of the applicants and the need of local authorities to have as full information as possible on the demand for council housing in their area. We therefore recommend that there should be no residential qualification for admission to housing lists. Indeed, we go further and hold it to be fundamental that no one should be precluded from applying for, or being considered for, a council tenancy on any ground whatsoever . . . . . We think that this rule should be made a statutory obligation."[15]

Fortunately the 1976 Race Relations Act made it unlawful to be denied housing simply on the grounds of being of non-British nationality. This only went part of the way suggested by the Cullingworth Committee which sought to remove all barriers to access to council tenancy lists except genuine housing needs. Nevertheless, the 1976 Race Relations Act may be helpful in breaking down another of the barriers – the residential qualification. Experience has shown that because of their housing circumstances Black people are frequently required to move more than the indigenous white population. This would make satisfying various residential requirements much more difficult. Since residential rules of this nature, which have no assessible "housing need" content may be shown to effect an identifiable community more than the rest they would certainly fall foul of the law on the issue of indirect discrimination.

ALLOCATIONS

But merely achieving access to council housing is not all. It is equally important that Blacks obtain a fair share of the quality housing that is available. As was pointed out in the case of access, local authorities have been weak in getting information across to potential users. Most of this work has been done in London. The Runnymede Trust report *Race and Council Housing in London* (1975), and subsequent research by the Community Relations Commission (1976) reveal a patchy situation, with some boroughs giving the ethnic minorities a fair share of newer housing while others were scarcely aware of the consequences of their own allocation procedures and the results achieved from them. Recently where both the London Borough of Islington and the Greater London Authority surveyed what was going on in their own services, they were led to the conclusion that Black families were getting the less favourable housing.

Five elements affect allocations and each is crucial to the final outcome. The available choice element in the full range of the rentable housing stock held by the local authority at any one time. Obviously what a family can get is ultimately limited by this, but real choice is further limited by the knowledge of opportunities of which the family is unaware. Lack of knowledge is therefore very significant in the way families respond and may be a function of how the lettings procedures actually work. Whether the letting procedures allow for the family to be given full information on the range of accommodation which meets their needs or whether such information is censored in any way and for any reason other than housing needs will affect the actual allocation.

The two remaining elements in allocation are largely in the hands of people outside the local authority as service deliverer. The would-be-tenant in exercising his preference may opt for a locality he knows, one that does not disrupt his friendship patterns, is advantageous for getting to and from work and generally presents the minimum of dislocation. His preference may in some instances accept second best because of other considerations. Housing Officials are likely to draw too generalised conclusions from the exercise of individual choice, and working on those assumptions limit the information passed on to others within the same racial group. The final element, transfers, can become skewed if white families beginning to fear the arrival of Black tenants on a particular estate suddenly increase the rate of transfers from that estate increasing the vacancies while decreasing them elsewhere.

The comments of the Working Party of Directors of Housing on two of these variables – available choice and knowledge of opportunities – should be noted –

"A new estate may become available for letting at the same time as an area of housing that is very multiracial is being cleared. In Manchester this resulted in many families from an established West Indian community being housed together on a deck access walk-up estate that has subsequently become unpopular, especially since the city had ceased to build to this

design in favour of low-rise housing. At the time there was no other housing available on the scale needed and in the areas that households wished to be.

"In some areas the size of distribution of dwellings may make equitable allocation difficult. In at least one London borough the larger dwellings frequently required by Black families are concentrated on older estates. This may be so in other areas.

"Households with New Commonwealth background are more likely to take the first option given them, possibly because they are less familiar with the system or because they are in worse housing conditions. White families, may hold out longer for alternative offers. The situation may become more acute if white families, worried by Black families moving in, start requesting transfer from these estates."[16]

PRIVATE SECTOR

From the evidence available the conclusion can be reached that the higher incidence of owner occupation among ethnic minority groups is due largely to the Asian communities. Owner-occupation among West Indians being nearer to that of the population as a whole. Unable for a variety of reasons to gain access to municipal housing and denied by racial discrimination access to private rented accommodation, early immigrants were forced into house purchasing. The majority of private rented accommodation being that supplied by other immigrants. This in many instances was at above average rates simply because the financing costs faced by the owners of the property for reasons the author will explain later.

It is interesting to note that in the Asian community owner-occupation increases the lower the socio-economic group of the head of household. This is in direct contrast to the white population. This is partly explained by the fact that the majority of the Asian community as compared with the West Indian community are found in areas of the UK where there has been and still is a stock of smaller cheap housing to buy.

The desire for house-ownership and the other pressures already referred to led Blacks to the lower end of the housing market where they became captives of high-priced money, oftimes including second and third mortgages, and low re-sale values which were rapidly being outpaced by inflation. The higher level of house ownership among Asians as compared with West Indians seem to arise from two reasons. One, the majority of Asians settle in areas of the UK where there is still a stock of smaller and cheaper houses to buy, and because of the closer cultural and kinship ties initial deposits were easier to obtain, several members in one family clubbing together to provide the deposit. In the West Indian community a more basic form of the Credit Union system, known as "The Hand"[17] provided the necessary deposits.

The policies concerned with the system of financing owner-occupation have tremendous significance for Black groups. The traditional way of financing home ownership, particularly for first-time buyers, is the Building Society. Whereas, 75 per cent of the white population acquire mortgages through Building Societies for owner-occupation less than one half of the Black population find owner-occupation through this source. Consequently, Blacks have drawn heavily on local authority funding. The figures in this respect speak for themselves – 39 per cent West Indians, 33 per cent Asians, 13 per cent other owners. Blacks are therefore sharply hit when local authority mortgages are in short supply. This is controlled by the amount of money Central Government allows a local authority to spend for this purpose in any one year.

One of the major factors which have restricted Blacks in the use of Building Societies is their reluctance to make loans on pre-1919 houses. Yet it is precisely in those areas of pre-1919 housing that nearly half of Black Britain lives. This is nearly twice the percentage of the white population living in those areas. As a result a large number of Blacks in an effort to solve their housing need have been forced to seek the help of fringe banks or in small companies, already referred to, for topping up loans, second and third mortgages. This has meant higher interest rates and higher than normal cumulative repayments. It is a classic example of the "colour tax" by which individuals face increased costs by virtue of their colour.

Black householders therefore often find themselves in areas where rehabilitation policies could help to improve their housing stocks and so raise the level of amenity. This is consistent with the Government view expressed in 1975: "The Government expected that most Housing Action Areas in the conurbations would, by their nature, be likely to include ethnic minorities."[18]

But in addition there is the factor of racial discrimination. In tests carried out in 1973, Smith found that in house-purchase tests Asian and West Indian applicants were discriminated against in 17 per cent of cases and in 27 per cent of cases when applying for rented accommodation. These findings were at early stages of the application; but there are obviously other opportunities for discrimination at later stages of the process.[19]

66

CONCENTRATION and DISPERSAL

Rex and Moore,[20] and Cullingworth[21] have assumed that ethnic concentrations are involuntary in the sense that immigrants are prevented from exercising choice by the presence of certain institutional and social barriers in white society which combine to restrict them to the working-class areas of residence. A study by the Community Relations Commission, however, came to the conclusion that ethnic concentrations are often voluntary and that some Black people have "some very positive reasons for their choice." While conceding that the areas in which most Blacks live are less desirable in their physical characteristics, it argued that they are generally more desirable in respect of certain amenities favoured by members of particular ethnic communities. The Commission therefore concluded:–

> *"Our view is that a viable housing policy should have two aims –*
> *the improvement of housing conditions in the areas of*
> *concentration and the furtherance of individual choice in housing*
> *by removing barriers to mobility."*[22]

The CRC view certainly begs the question of why those amenities could not be found or provided elsewhere. Nor does it go any way towards answering the views of Rex and Moore together with those of Cullingworth. Indeed the majority of Black concentration is the result of the combination of "white flight", white people selling up and leaving an area as Blacks come in – thus leaving more accommodation for Blacks to buy in those areas; and racial discrimination, on the one hand making it near impossible for Blacks to gain access to certain areas whether in the private or public sector and on the other creating a feeling of isolation amongst Blacks and thus the need to stick together. Besides, since racial discrimination has contributed in a major way to keeping Blacks in the lower economic strata it has denied them the finance for upward mobility in the housing market and as had been pointed out even when the money is there, the policies of the supplying agents and their allies have mitigated against this process.

Data available from inner area studies reveals that there has been little movement from areas of original settlement, although there has been some considerable movement within those areas. There is nothing local authorities can do about concentration in the private sector and any measures designed purely to disperse communities would fall foul of the Race Relations Act.[23] Yet it was only in 1968 that the Cullingworth Committee in its final recommendation to local authorities had this to say:–

"Dispersal is a laudable aim of policy, but this policy needs pursuing with full respect for the wishes of the people concerned. Dispersal of immigrant concentration should be regarded as a desirable consequence, but not the overriding purpose of housing individual immigrant families on council states. The criteria of full, informed, individual choice comes first."[24]

The over-riding political impetus for dispersal is fear. It has nothing to do with housing needs of Blacks. It is the simple realisation that if Blacks remain trapped in specific housing areas they would eventually turn to the more articulate among them and whether the major political parties wanted it or not, seek political representation. Dispersal was therefore not being pushed in the interest of Blacks but as an expedient in the process of retaining white dominance.

COMMUNICATING with MINORITIES

Society has decided that a certain minimum level of education is desirable for all citizens and has set about ensuring its provision for every child as of right. It has made no such determination on housing and although it has placed a responsibility on local authorities to deal with homelessness when it arises there is no national strategy of home provision. The provision of housing therefore remains a reflection of the current free market forces and local political sensitivity to housing needs. The complex of legal, financial and administrative procedures that have as a result developed can prove bewildering even to the well informed.

Many local authorities, have in an effort to improve communication with the public at large set up housing and advice centres to assist the public in understanding the plethora of schemes which exist and the criteria for eligibility and selection under the various schemes, their advantages, the relative time lag and other related matters.

But in so doing not all authorities have recognised the need to overcome the language barrier which certain groups still experience. While this is most obvious in Asian and Cypriot households, there are still residual problems with West Indian households. The Working Party of Housing Directors summed up the problem this way:–

"The difficulties of getting housing information across to the community at large has been generally recognised for some time, and the setting up of housing aid and advice centres has been seen as one solution to this communication problem. Ethnic

minorities share with the rest of the community all the difficulties of finding out about and understanding the complex legal, financial and administrative procedures involved in the housing market. In addition, some may have extra difficulties which compound the problem of finding out how to obtain satisfactory housing. The main additional difficulty is the language barrier – this is obvious in the case of Asian and Cypriot households. But cultural differences can also give rise to serious misunderstandings."[25]

RECORD KEEPING

The argument on record-keeping in housing has swung to and fro as it has in other areas of service delivery. There are those who object to record keeping out of a strong moral conviction that colour is irrelevant to service delivery. Others object because they see it as an assault on their professional integrity, their commitment to objectivity and fair play. Yet at the end of the day, the only safe management tool is neither faith nor hope, but an adequate data base.

The Cullingworth Committee received a body of views against the idea of keeping records of Black people, saying that this was both morally repugnant and could lead to discriminatory practices. It subsequently concluded that record keeping was an essential tool of management agreeing that only if one knew the details of a situation could one hope to tackle the problems which arose. The Committee reported:–

"We think there is much confusion of this issue. To maintain that colour is irrelevant is to treat a moral axiom as if it were a fact: what is, can be very different from what should be. Colour is not irrelevant, as we have demonstrated throughout . . . The very fact that discrimination is so frequently unintentional strongly supports the case for keeping records. They enable a local authority to satisfy itself that it is not following policies which lead to the very discrimination it wishes to avoid.

"Adequate records are essential not merely to counter charges of discrimination and to demonstrate that justice is being done but also as an integral part of management and policy formulation. They also enable the larger local authorities to establish that their intended policies are in fact being implemented at every level in the administrative hierarchy. We therefore recommend that records should be kept and used."[26]

The Government White Paper in 1975 was less forthright,

although it did see ethnic record keeping as part of a wider data base. It put its case this way:–

". . . the Government believes that local authorities should seek to assemble, within current restraints on staff and money, the best information they at present can about the range of housing problems in their area, including the problems of the various groups whose needs are in one or another special, and against whom, for lack of knowledge, there may be unintentional discrimination. In its view, the collection of relevant information about the housing situation and needs of coloured people should form part of authorities' wider arrangements for understanding and dealing with the housing and social problems of their area, and for housing management purposes; it will show how social problems are inter-related in central areas. Comprehensive and detailed information, which can be employed by authorities to determine the policies and the action required in their area, will be more useful in bringing about results than concentrating on formal records by reference to colour alone, distinct from need."[27]

The mere keeping of records is useless unless there is a monitoring system to ensure that the policies to which the record keeping gives rise are understood and implemented at every level throughout the organisation. It is pointless having a tool, if there is neither the intention nor the will to use. But it is tragic to assume that the job can be done without adequate tools. It is unfortunate, therefore, that so far Central Government has given only lukewarm support to the call for adequate record keeping.

HOUSING ASSOCIATIONS

This is a growing voluntary movement some way between public and private housing. The Cullingworth Committee had excluded Housing Associations from its remit since they were part of the work of another committee (the Cohen Committee) which unfortunately proved abortive. The Department of the Environment's Housing Advisory Group, in its study of "Housing Associations and their part in Current Housing Strategies" in 1979, failed to see the importance of the voluntary movement in the achievement of racial equality and its advice subsequently ignored allocation policies altogether.

However, Fox argues that Housing Associations should now be a significant element of the housing market for ethnic groups and their development should be included in local authorities' own Housing

70

Investment Programmes and strategies. He contends that most Housing Associations are better equipped to deal with that part of ethnic housing needs which require greater service and support than given in normal council housing, eg homeless Black youth, lone mother and baby, elderly Asian, battered women. Indeed some Housing Associations are already specialising in such needs.[28]

RACIAL DISCRIMINATION in HOUSING

Discrimination has been shown by Smith to be practised against Asians and West Indians in both house purchase and house rentals. Even in the initial stage of application he was able to demonstrate discrimination in 17 per cent of applicants seeking house purchase and 27 per cent of those seeking rented accommodation. Smith was quick to point out that his tests were at early stages of the application and that other opportunities to discriminate exist at other stages in the process.

The Commission for Racial Equality has been involved in litigation with residents who under the 1976 Race Relations Act have been guilty of discrimination through applying pressure, on their neighbours not to sell to Blacks. But this type of pressure, sometimes in the form of inducement through the offer of a higher price for the property, very seldom comes to notice. On one occasion which came to light, the individuals told the Court that all they had done was convene a community relations meeting to see how best they could welcome the Asian family into their community. This so impressed the learned judge that he dismissed the case even though the persons who convened the meeting for those noble objectives suddenly found next day that their son who was living abroad was returning to England, needed somewhere to live and was led to spend a recent legacy on buying the house for cash and at a price 5 per cent higher than that previously agreed with the Asian family.

There is no facet of the housing market, private or public that is not affected by racial discrimination. Since housing is so much a result of political decision-making and the money market, only as Blacks gain power in these two areas can they hope to achieve any favourable results.

"For the child of the immigrant it is particularly difficult to retain a coherence sense of identity. Those who have his care have a special responsibility to provide an environment where a dual culture, like bilingualism is a positive factor"

HMSO. *Foster Care – A Guide to Practice*
London. DHSS – 1976, page 44

Chapter 5
Does Social Work Have The Answer

ETHNIC MINORITIES and the SOCIAL SERVICES

The Social Services Department may be described as the place where the disadvantaged meet. When one adds Black ethnic minorities to the situation and then brings in those discriminated against on the grounds of their race, colour, or ethnic origins, the result is racial discrimination and disadvantage meeting. Can the services cope with this new dimension? Many people would argue that the services are unable to cope, but the most disturbing feature is the underlying reasons for their inability to cope. It is the failure to accept the role of racial discrimination as it affects training, administration and service delivery that has rendered the service near impotent in dealing with this challenge in certain areas.

Roger Ballard takes the position that although there are now substantial Asian and West Indian settlements in most major cities, the issues posed for the Social Services by their presence are still being approached with uncertainty.[1] Much of the literature still perpetuates the concept of "immigrant" describing cultural and social backgrounds, their reasons for immigrating to Britain and problems of adjustment in the new environment. The works of Cheetham[2] (1972), currently a member of the Commission for Racial Equality, Jones[3] (1976) and Triseliotis[4] (1972) are illustrations of that approach.

Ballard argues that the earlier assumption that the cultural distinctiveness of members of the minority groups would gradually fade and that the behaviour of their children would closely resemble that of the host population has not been realised and that a straightforward process of assimilation is not taking place. He finds little in the training of practitioners – social workers, probation

72

officers and others – which would prepare them for their task of working with members of ethnic minority groups.

Certainly Cheetham, Jones and others have pursued the line that if only one could appreciate the cultural and social backgrounds of Blacks and their reasons for coming to Britain, then one could deal with the problems of adjustment posed by the society and thus take the problems in hand. What Cheetham and others have failed to accept is the fact that the main force resisting the development of the knowledge they are advocating is the level of racial prejudice in the total society.

The logical extension of that theory as expressed by Ballard is that with time the cultural distinctiveness of the Black community would fade as more and more of their children were born here and brought up entirely in British schools. For a variety of reasons, not least the need of the Black communities to protect themselves, this expected assimilation has not taken place.

While gaining some understanding of the forces at play and thus developing an insight into and sensitivity about the life-styles and value systems of ethnic minorities in modern society will enhance the quality of social work for ethnic minority clients it is basic to all social work delivery to all clients. Over and above that general point, it is crucial to appreciate the fact that Black people suffer seriously from added deprivation resulting from racial discrimination by the society as a whole. In addition to all that, as a result of the ethno-centrism of the vast majority of Social Services they tend to operate from a position of cultural superiority and fail to appreciate the cultural and religious differences of some groups and the difficult dilemmas to which these differences give rise.

As Ballard pointed out, there is little in the training of social workers to prepare them for their work with Black communities. But this failure to train stems from the reluctance to admit a problem that stares the services in the face. The Social Services agencies have prided themselves in providing a personal service.

It is worthy of note therefore that Cheetham, following a visit to the USA as part of a research project sponsored by the Department of Health and Social Security in which she was looking at Social Work practices in the USA and Britain, has redressed the balance somewhat. The resulting book "Social Work and Ethnicity" does recognise, in a way social work practice has hitherto failed to acknowledge, the role of racial discrimination and disadvantage in inhibiting service delivery. Future generations of social work students will thus be better served.

Cross, in his study of the Inner City looked at the extent to which social services have responded or failed to respond to the presence of ethnic minorities in urban areas; the extent to which these groups were disadvantaged in gaining access to those services which are relevant to their needs and the extent to which their needs were the same as or were different from those of the indigenous population.[5]

He further contends that the relationship of ethnic minority group members to the social services is determined by two important considerations. Firstly, in contrast to educational and health services, the social services are not provided universally for the whole population regardless of need. They are in fact only offered to that sector of the population, a minority, who exhibit their need for support and assistance by the conditions in which they live or by the problems which they experience. Some of the people identified as clients of the social services are in constant need of assistance while others, normally self-sufficient, need assistance only during periods of crisis such as death or illness.

Secondly, because the philosophy of the service is one of a personal service which assesses and meets individual needs, social services departments have been reluctant to identify their clients in terms of their racial or religious backgrounds. Instead, they tend to group their clients in accordance with shared disadvantage, hence single-parent families, the disabled. Thus grouping follows rather than precedes need identification.

Since being Black cannot in itself be a deprivation, "decision-makers" within the services have been faced with the problem of identification of those needs and deprivations which arise from causes different from those for which their traditional casework context has provided a framework and for which the symptoms follow a new and uncharted course.

"Decision-makers" interviewed by Cross et al, expressed the situation in the following terms by three different respondents:–

(1) "We have coloured old people in homes for the aged, but no homes specifically for coloured old people.

(2) "We make provision for problems that arise among groups. If these problems arise within a particular ethnic group, then within the case context, we shall look at them. I don't think we ever really consider problems as being particular to particular ethnic groups. If this does occur, then we will try to make adequate provision but we don't say: 'Well we have

a Black problem; we must now make provision for that problem'."

(3) "We do not make special exceptions for immigrants or treat them as a special group. We are concerned to improve our services and make them more relevant to the socially deprived as a whole and that includes immigrants."[6]

A Working Party of the Association of Directors of Social Services, accepting the over-representation of ethnic minority groups in the most disadvantaged groups in society and the mounting evidence of the wide extent of both racial discrimination and racial disadvantage, have made a plea for social services departments to give special thought to their work with ethnic minority groups because of the particular dimension of need caused by newness, cultural differences and racial prejudice and discrimination. They felt that this involved three separate approaches: firstly, a review of need to evaluate how far policies and strategies were meeting the needs of ethnic and other minorities; secondly, use of their experience in dealing with outside bodies to ensure a co-ordinated, comprehensive and relevant approach among public and voluntary agencies in respect of work in the multi-racial field; and thirdly, influence the local authority through corporate or other management structures to set up the appropriate machinery to promote good race relations practice.[7]

SOME SPECIAL NEEDS

Pyke-Lees and Gardner[8] in their study of ethnic elderly, tried to set out the different set of difficulties experienced by the ethnic elderly over and above those which they share with the rest of society. Firstly, there is insecurity in the new environment occasioned by remoteness from friends and relations, their different cultural background and the consequent difficulty in establishing new neighbourhood and community networks to replace those lost through immigration. Secondly, the whole syndrome of isolation and rejection occasioned by racial discrimination and prejudice. Thirdly, those difficulties which arise from the contrast between expectation of care they would have received within their families in their home country and the realities of care in Britain and finally the loss of status and role in the family and in society as family patterns adjust to conditions in Britain.

According to the 1971 Census there were 26,400 elderly persons from the New Commonwealth living in Britain. The figure does not

75

include elderly refugees from Uganda and Cyprus. From the general demographic distribution of Blacks this number is bound to continue rising for some time.

Table 9
Elderly People from Ethnic Minorities

	Men	Women	Total
New Commonwealth	14,000	12,400	26,400
India	6,700	4,900	11,600
Pakistan	1,200	200	1,400
West Indies	3,300	3,300	6,600
Cyprus	1,600	1,400	3,000
Africa	500	400	900

Source: Cross. Op cit, page 124

When looking at the special needs of Black Britain, the ethnic elderly come close to the top of the list for two reasons. Firstly, they constitute a hidden problem because of declining mobility which takes them out of sight, and secondly, a false but none-the-less widely held view that because they have not been making demands on the social services they have been adequately cared for within their own communities. This latter belief results frm a general failure to appreciate the extent to which the extended family structure has given way under the pressures of life in Britain.

It is worth noting the arguments put forward by Pyke-Lees and Gardiner in respect of the growing number of Black elderly who spent their childhood and first part or major part of their adult life in their country of origin and thus acquired strong cultural roots. But it must be stressed that it would be folly to assume that as Blacks who were born here grow old that all will be well. One merely has to follow the fortunes of the elderly Blacks of Cardiff and Liverpool, two seaport cities with several generations of Black settlement, to realise that they still experience the whole syndrome of isolation, rejection and unfulfilled ambitions occasioned by racial discrimination and prejudice.

Another area of special need is that of the one-parent family. In the early 1970s there were proportionately more one-parent families in the West Indian community. While this is still true, the rate of increase within the Asian community is growing and the gap between the West Indian and Asian communities narrows slowly.

Hood et al in their Paddington study found that 65 per cent of

West Indian mothers were married and 14 per cent were in a stable cohabitation.[9] Moody and Stroud[10], using a sample of 100 found that 85 were married, while Pollack in the Brixton study found 73 per cent of West Indian mothers were married and 17 per cent were in stable cohabitation, while only 10 per cent were living alone.[11]

Hunt's survey of one-parent families in the London Borough of Haringey showed that 20 per cent of unmarried mothers were West Indians at a time when West Indians constituted only 10 per cent of two-parent families. What was interesting however, was that the survey also showed that the reason for this over-representation of West Indian one-parent families was not a higher rate of marital breakdown but to the existence of a larger number of unmarried, never married, West Indian mothers.[12]

A joint circular from the Department of Health and Social Services (DHSS) and the Department of Education and Science (DES) states that "in providing services for disadvantaged children from ethnic minorities, local authorities should consider how their services and the way they are presented need to be modified to take account of linguistic and cultural differences.[13] OPCS figures reveal that 6-7 per cent of all children born in Britain today have mothers who were born in the New Commonwealth. However, in 14 boroughs over 25 per cent of all the births are in this category and in a further 28 boroughs the percentage is over 15 per cent.

Lomas and Monck in their Runneymede Trust Census Study revealed that in Leicester 85 per cent of "coloured" mothers of children under five were at work. In Manchester it was 77 per cent, in Bradford 44 per cent and in Wolverhampton 41 per cent. This compared with a national average of 50 per cent for all mothers of children under five. The majority of white mothers worked less than 30 hours per week, but in Bradford, Leicester and Manchester 75 per cent of the coloured mothers worked over 30 hours a week.[14] This pointed to clear indications of greater need for ethnic minority families for day care assistance. This is the third area of special need.

But the evidence extracted from the Census data by the Runneymede Trust illustrates that not only does a higher percentage of Black mothers as compared with white mothers go to work, but that they work much longer hours. Because of the long working hours, such responses like pre-school playgroups and nursery school classes are less of an answer to their needs, and their demands are for greater day care facilities. The inability or failure of the local authority to meet this need has sustained the higher level of unregistered child minders in the Black communities.

For years social work agencies built up a theory on the social consequences of immigration which explained away their ineffectiveness in dealing with children of West Indian families. The syndrome which was supposed to have had disproportionate numbers of West Indian children into residential care in community homes or penal institutions like detention centres and approved schools was related to their late immigration, separation from their families and consequent rejection by their natural parents. The simplistic theory built up in the 1960s has been severely undermined by the growing numbers of children of West Indian origin who are born in Britain and who are now finding themselves in care. It is becoming clear that the syndrome identified in the 1960s was only part of the picture and that in an environment hostile to Blacks, alienation amongst the young at the most deprived end of the scale is bound to result.

It is impossible to overemphasize the need for social agencies to recognise how society has, through prejudices and discrimination, destroyed Black confidence and self-esteem and denied many Black youth of their right to work as well as their right to acquire by legitimate means the ordinary things of life. It is at this point that we must look for a lot of the alienation exhibited among Black youth today.

A piece of research carried out in Approved Schools in 1971 showed that the Black boys committed to them had less serious offence histories than was usual for boys committed to Approved Schools. The report stated:–

"Whatever did account for the early committal of Black boys we have been unsuccessful in isolating it. However, in the absence of any clear link with home background or behavioural characteristics, it is hard indeed to see any alternative explanation to racial prejudice as the cause of the situation."[15]

Commenting on the research results the Working Party of Directors of Social Services said that it had commonly been believed and oftimes stated that the main problems of West Indian children related to their immigration, separation from their families and consequent rejection by their natural parents but that Cawson and others have shown this not to be the case.[16] Indeed, Cawson has shown that 37 per cent of the boys and 43 per cent of the girls from ethnic groups in Approved Schools were born in Britain. A further 21 per cent of boys and 6 per cent of girls had been in Britain for less than two years and had accompanied either one or both parents when coming to Britain. A survey carried out in the West Midlands by the West Midlands Children Regional Planning Centre, revealed that 26 per cent of the Black children in community homes were born in Jamaica and 66 per cent were born in Britain.[17]

Peter Warren, in his study of four years work with clients of West Indian origin and descent in the Probation Service, has this to say:—

"The most serious social concern arising from the presence of ethnic minorities in Britain is the increasing number of youths of West Indian origin or descent who are becoming alienated from society and falling into crime. One particular aspect of this is the 'crime' which seems to involve no evidence other than that of the police, such as assault on the police, threatening words and behaviour and (particularly in London) 'SUS' – being a suspected person. The whole problem has been largely ignored by social work agencies but is now expressed as a major concern by police in London, Birmingham and other areas of West Indian settlement."[18]

But he is even more strident when he describes the consequences of this failure on the Black youth themselves:—

"For twenty years children of West Indian parents have been taken away from home by local authorities and placed in residential schools and homes where they have felt even less secure than at home, and have had even less opportunity or encouragement to value themselves as Black people. The Courts have sentenced Black youths to Detention Centres and Borstals where again, they cannot identify with their environment, except in a negative way. The Probation and After-Care Service, charged with the supervision of people discharged from penal establishments in addition to those placed on probation by the Courts has, like the Social Services Departments failed to recognise the speciality of the Black youth in social work terms. The employment situation has become grave, with prejudice and discrimination of a most covert kind ensuring that young Blacks are at the bottom of the unemployment pile. Thus they are denied the right to work and the right to acquire by legitimate means the ordinary everyday requisites of life such as reasonable accommodation, reasonable clothing and reasonable leisure activities. They develop the attitude that if no one cares for them, why should they care for anybody else."[19]

Two other special needs are worth noting. There are those associated with adoption and those relating to mental health. On the first of these there is both the problem of finding Black couples who are prepared to adopt or foster other people's children, as well as getting them accepted by the appropriate agencies when these are willing and prepared to accept this responsibility. In the first instance a number of cultural and religious mores relating to the role and responsibility of parenthood, and the higher level of community expectation may make Black couples reluctant in coming forward. But in the second case their lower socio-economic status and different cultural orientation may pose difficulties for the assessors of the adoption and fostering agencies who are accustomed to making their judgement from within different social criteria.

Despite DHSS guidance and efforts by Black professionals to deal with both aspects of the problem there is still a great deal to be done to bridge the gap, particularly for those children whose natural parents were of different races.

The Association of British Adoption and Fostering Agencies (ABAFA) have produced two booklets for those contemplating the adoption of Black children. The first is titled *Adopting a Black Child* and the second is called *Inter-Racial Adoption*. These have been backed up by a publication by the CRE called *Fostering Black Children*. The DHSS in guidance on caring for children from different cultures says: –

"The ability to hold on to a true sense of their own identity is needed by all children who experience separation from their parents. For the child of the immigrant it is particularly difficult to retain a coherent sense of identity. Those who share his care have a special responsibility to provide an environment where a dual culture, like bilingualism is a positive factor.[20]

A special campaign, known as The Soul Kids Campaign, was an attempt by a group of informed Black professionals to stimulate and recruit foster parents from within the Black community. The Adoption Resource Exchange and Independent Adoption Society were associated with this effort. In 1976 out of 124 children placed by Adoption Resource Exchange, 55 were West Indian, 22 were Asian and 57 Caucasian and others.[21]

Nowhere is the challenge to social workers as great as it is in the mental health field. Not only is the client likely to be experiencing the stresses of living in a sophisticated modern society, but also those resulting from his having come from a more pedestrian one. Added to those, however, are the stresses created by prejudice and discrimination. These cumulative pressures are more acutely experienced by the adolescents of all groups and the women in the

Asian communities, many of whom may not only lack the support of the extended family but may also be experiencing communication difficulties.

Here traditional social work practice has to decide whether the perceived behaviour patterns are normal within the context of the minority culture or symptomatic of dysfunction brought on by the situation of stress. It must also determine whether the behaviour is individual to the extent of being beyond the control of family or community support, always bearing in mind that owing to communication difficulties and group pride as well as the taboo that surrounds mental illness in many cultures, appeals for help are only made at the moment of extreme crisis. There is also a failure to understand what facilities are available and how to gain access to them.

Any correct diagnosis depends upon an appreciation of the psycho-social stress to which the individual is exposed. Because ethnicity is a crucial factor in diagnosis and treatment it is important that social workers recognise the extent to which a task already requiring highly developed skills within their own cultural group can become immensely more complicated by the dimension of other cultures.

Dr Philip Rack, in his discussion of Asians and the psychiatric services in Lynfield Mount Hospital in Bradford, concludes:–

"Cultural factors affect mental illness in many ways. The psychoses occur in all cultures, but there are differences in the symptoms which they produce. Neuroses and other stress actions also vary, and correct diagnosis depends on an understanding of the psycho-social stresses to which the individual is exposed.

"Most industrial centres in the developed world are to some extent multi-cultural and it is essential that psychiatrists and other health workers should recognise this cultural diversity and its clinical consequences. The Asian population of Bradford provides an example of this. There are probably just as many important differences in the mental health problems of other minority groups in other places."[22]

COMMUNITY and FAMILY SUPPORT

One of the strengths of the Black community has always been its tendency towards self-reliance and self-help. Unfortunately agencies have not been quick enough to exploit this strength and have been more anxious to condemn its failings than develop its strengths. In the same way the social worker does not always understand or appreciate his clients needs because of the cultural gap, so too, the

81

community in attempting to give support does not always understand or appreciate the role of the social work agency with whom it should be in contact.

A study by the Community Relations Commission revealed a free or cheap form of child care through the use of husbands, grand-parents and other relatives, but there were some marked group differences. One in three white and West Indian mothers used their husbands, working on a different work shift to their own, while less than one in five Asian mothers used that method. On the other hand, Asian mothers used grand-parents and other relatives almost twice as frequently as white and West Indian mothers.[23]

Another study by the Community Relations Commission showed that Black people were less aware of agencies which could help them than their white counterparts – four in ten Black respondents compared to eight in ten white respondents being aware of the appropriate facilities, even though there was some difference in the degree to which they felt they needed advice. Thirty-nine per cent of the indigenous sample felt they had been in a position where they needed advice compared with 42 per cent of West Indians, 43 per cent of the Cypriots, 32 per cent of Pakistanis, 30 per cent of the Indians and 28 per cent of the East African Asians.[24]

A further example of the strong self-reliance and community support of the Asian, and in particular the East African Asian, is given in the results of the Community Relations Commission's study of the settlement of Ugandan Asians. In order to handle the re-settlement the Government set up the Uganda Settlement Board; of the 28,000 who arrived in Britain for re-settlement, some 7,000, i.e. 25 per cent did not go through the Board at all, but used the community and family support system. Of the 21,000 who went initially to one of the Board's reception centres, some 10,000, nearly half, again used the community network to achieve their own settlement. The Board and its auspices settled the remaining 11,000. What is perhaps more important is the fact that those who depended on community support did better by way of finding jobs, housing, schools and other amenities in addition to having the personal friendships and support needed to rebuild their confidence after the trauma of evacuation.[25]

The Working Party of Directors of Social Services summed up the need for community involvement by saying that self-help as a strategy should be supported by local authorities for two reasons. Firstly, existing services were stretched and authorities often found it difficult to cope, and secondly minority groups had special needs and young people in particular often needed identity models from their own ethnic groups.[26]

It must be borne in mind that necessity rather than anything else is the strongest 'push' factor in the development of a number of self-help agencies which have sprung up to cope with a variety of situations from child-care to community support and consulting groups. Despite the strong cultural mores associated with family support, a lot of what still flourishes in the community is the result of failure to adjust adequately to existing services.

While believing strongly that self-help groups should be supported because once properly organised and run they give the community a bigger stake in finding and determining answers to its own identified needs, the author is wary of the reasons offered by the Working Party of Directors of Social Services for supporting self-help as a strategy. In the first intance what some local authorities were doing was nothing beyond passing their responsibility over to willing but unqualified and badly equipped community groups and asking the groups to provide a service on the cheap. This can in no way be described as a positive strategy towards self-help. It cannot be denied that minority groups need identity models from their own ethnic group, but we must ensure that these models are success models. Few local authorities are providing self-help groups with the level of support necessary to ensure success models and failure models only reinforce the concepts of inferiority and feed the consequences of racial prejudice.

STAFFING and TRAINING

Although administrators are quick to lament the absence or scarcity of Black staff, few are prepared to take any positive steps to remedy the situation. Here the concept of identity models reoccurs. The presence of Black social workers in the agency is bound in most cases to have the effect on the Black client that the agency is able to understand his point of view. It removes the image of ethnocentrism from the agency and provides it with a broader contact base for doing its work. This does not mean that only Black social workers can understand and cope with Black clients, but contends that the ethos of a personal service that represents that of its clients group is bound to have a head start in credibility.

All the evidence is that training agencies have been slow to respond to the needs of the service in so far as work in a multi-racial society is concern, and managers have not always been

83

imaginative enough in adapting in-service training to these needs for fear of not being able to cope with the dormant racial prejudices that might be unleashed.

In an unpublished report by Lynda Baker and Charles Husband of Leicester University School of Social Work, some light is thrown on the response of training courses to the demands of a multiracial society. Responses were received from 92 of the 120 colleges approached. Sixtynine per cent of respondents had no compulsory element in their main qualifying courses and 7 per cent had no teaching at all in the area. Fifty per cent of respondents offered only superficial teaching, some through special elective courses and the rest through main-stream work or fieldwork placements.[27]

The Working Party of Directors accepted that while it was ultimately desirable for all qualifying courses to have a race relations input, for the immediate future emphasis would have to be on in-service training. They offered three general reasons. Firstly, teachers on current qualifying courses felt that there was already too much in an overcrowded syllabus; secondly, workers were more likely to be motivated for such training if they were experiencing difficulties in their work; and thirdly, worker mobility would increase the need for more social workers to be informed about minority groups. They contended that training for work in multiracial areas should be given to all social service staff whom they classified in three groups:– (a) those who have face-to-face contact with minority ethnic groups, eg nursery nurses, social workers, home helps, receptionists; (b) those who provide a personal service or share a home with members of minority groups, eg house-parents, foster parents and care staff; and (c) policy makers who define priorities and allocate resources.[28]

A firm knowledge base is essential since it is impossible to begin to work effectively with clients without some understanding of the cultural values held by the particular ethnic group to which the client belongs. This is even more important when it is likely that those values may be in conflict with values held dear to the social worker. It is equally necessary for trainers to pursue a close examination of social work methods to ensure that these are modified to take account of the needs and values of ethnic minority group clients and that approaches to be used are suitable for multi-cultural situations. Students should always be made aware of special needs of Black groups and how these can be identified together with the channels open to them for communication with the community.

Social work agencies must be aware that some considerable part of the disadvantage which their Black clients suffer will spring from discrimination and prejudice. It is therefore important that they understand how it functions and how it affects the relationship between them and their clients, between one group of clients and another group of clients, them and their colleagues, them and their supervisors. Indeed that the whole complex of relationships which make up the service is constantly being called upon to face up to it.

Cross reported that decision-makers could deplore the general scarcity of well-trained staff who could operate with both ethnic minority and indigenous clients. They could recognise that the presence of ethnic minority clients has implications for the skills required by their staff but would reject specific and separate policy action. They could recognise the need to recruit social workers with an understanding of the background and problems of ethnic minority clients, and they could also recognise that the approach adopted by their staff in respect of ethnic minority clients might have to differ significantly from that used for an indigenous client. But despite all that, few adopted special measures to recruit appropriate staff. Most would recoil at the suggestion that their inaction amounted to the most subtle form of racial discrimination.

A few of the responses of decision-makers will illustrate the dichotomy:–

"I think one always hopes that one is going to be able to recruit people who have more understanding of the problems of ethnic minorities particularly with respect of the care of children. One attempts to do this, but I don't think we specifically advertise on those kind of terms. We have definitely not considered measures to this end and I don't think we are likely to do so. If there was a position being advertised, it would be advertised and we would appoint the best possible applicant for the job; if that applicant happens to be a member of an ethnic minority, then so be it."

"Asian or West Indian clients do not always like to have an Asian or West Indian social worker dealing with them. They don't like to be treated differently. I think it is better to have good training for regularly appointed staff rather than to recruit special staff for immigrant clients."

"It's all very well and fine in theory but once you start embarking on a policy of discriminating among social workers on the grounds of either their colour or the colour of their clients, all sorts of implications come in. I personally believe that we shall

get all the ethnic social workers we need in the course of time because of the composition of our borough. That will happen anyway and will improve things."

"I don't think that the general run of our social workers is adequately informed about the cultural background and needs of ethnic minority clients as they are about our indigenous ones."[29]

CASEWORK VERSUS COMMUNITY WORK

Casework practice has been developed upon a multi-faceted conceptual base some of which can be adapted easily to meet ethnic minority group needs. Depending on the knowledge base of the social worker, systems theory, role theory and learning theory would appear to be of some benefit in approaching case work with Black clients. Owing to the cultural gap, some other theories like family theory, client-centred therapy and psycho-analysis theory may require considerable, if impossible, modification and many will have to give way to some other form of working.

There is considerable difference of opinion in respect of the most appropriate help social workers can offer to the Black client. Holman doubts the usefulness of casework and asks the question:– "Is casework applicable to non-European attitudes?"[30]

John Rea-Price is adamant that casework principles apply equally to Blacks and whites and rejoices almost that no casework theorist has so far felt the urge to emulate the American author of *Text Book of Negro Casework.*[31]

Katrine Fitz-Herbert contends that the casework idiom of heart-to-heart talks, discussions of feelings and joint working out of rational plans is ineffective with clients unfamiliar with the conventional social worker role.[32] and Triseliotis comes down strongly in favour of group work because of the pattern of living associated with extended families.[33]

McCullock and Kornreich, however, put forward the case that since most of the problems of Black clients are engendered by the underlying structural inequalities in British society, any attempts to alleviate those problems on a case to case basis, using traditional casework techniques could be ineffective unless accompanied by "basic structural changes and positive discrimination within the wider society.[34]

This view is clearly on the ascendency. It is certainly nearer to the feelings of the Black community, but some administrators may have clutched upon it as an alibi for their own failure arguing that the failure in basic structural change rests elsewhere.

"There is enough experience in the Commonwealth to prove that harmony between races on a basis of partnership is a practical policy. We believe the mingling of culture leads to a richer and better society."

Conservative Political Centre
Wind of Change, 1960

Chapter 6

The Politics of Race and the Black Response

MAINSTREAM POLITICAL VIEWS

Following the end of World War II, Britain was faced with the task of rebuilding and reshaping its industrial strategy. Much of Western Europe, aided by the Marshall Plan, was replacing bombed-out factories with new and modern machines. By and large, Britain returned to old factories and labour intensive techniques, and was badly in need of unskilled and semi-skilled manpower. The colonies became a natural hunting ground, especially as many colonial people had volunteered and served in the various branches of the forces during the war.

Unfortunately, although the industrial machine needed the manpower it was the local authority, not the factory owner, who was responsible for supplying the schools, houses and other social amenities. There was no coherent migrant strategy and as early as 1954 Patrick Gordon Walker, a Labour MP, one of the first men in British politics to advocate control of Commonwealth immigration, was arguing that no country had a moral obligation to import a racial problem. Yet attempting to look both ways he avowed that he could not support an immigration policy that was based on colour. Addressing a constituency meeting in Smethwick on 12th November 1954 he said:–

"I don't think any country has a moral obligation to import a racial problem, but at the same time I would not support any immigration policy based on colour. I am a great believer in Commonwealth unity, but I cannot see that there will be any danger to it if Britain takes power over immigration. Every other country regulates immigration from other parts of the Commonwealth, including Britain."[1]

Foot points out that seven years later, Gordon Walker made one of the best speeches of his life while opposing the second reading of the Commonwealth Immigrants Bill 1962. He argued then that the Tory Bill "removed from Commonwealth citizens the long-standing right of free entry to Britain, and is thus calculated to undermine the unity and strength of the Commonwealth."[2] But by 1964 when he was contesting the Smethwick seat against Peter Griffiths (Tory) the Labour Party issued a special election leaflet on his behalf. It said:—

"Be fair."

"Immigrants only arrived in Smethwick in large numbers during the past ten years – while the Tory Government was in power. You can't blame Labour or Gordon Walker for that."

"Labour favours continued control of immigration, stricter health checks and deportation of those convicted of criminal offences. Labour will give local authorities greater power to help overcrowding. Labour will provide new and better housing."[3]

Foot observes that Gordon Walker's retreat from a principled stand on the immigration issue into opportunism was largely his own decision. But he was helped by his supporters in the local Labour Party. Indeed, several local councillors had, at one time or another been responsible for statements on immigration which were not in keeping with their party's (or their union's) official line. Even Ron Badham, who later became secretary of the local Labour Party, had fought a municipal by-election on the platform of a complete ban on immigration.[4]

Throughout the years, however liberal the Labour Party's official policy on race and immigration has been, there have been those amongst its ranks both high and low, who have responded to the gut reaction of racism in the society. Gaitskill had opposed the Commonwealth Immigrants Bill 1962, Wilson had greeted Peter Griffith's arrival at the House of Commons by dubbing him a "parliamentary leper" and Roy Jenkins had extolled the virtues of integration, yet in the May 1976 debate in the House of Commons, Bob Mellish a former Labour Chief Whip could say:—

"With 53 million of us, we cannot go on without strict control of immigration. People cannot come here just because they have a British passport – full stop . . . . enough is enough."[5]

In the same debate, Roy Jenkins, then Labour Home Secretary of the day, and now the leader of the new Social Democratic Party, enunciated what had, by the late 1970s, come to be the consensus among the three major political parties, Labour, Tory and Liberal:—

". . . an absolutely firm and determined front . . . against any form of discrimination within our society, accompanied by the recognition that there is a clear limit to the amount of immigration this country can absorb. That being so, the maintenance of a strict control is very much in the interests not only of the majority but the minorities."[6]

Two of the Tory spokesmen in that debate placed their variation on the theme. William Whitelaw talked of the "closely linked problems of immigration from the New Commonwealth and race relations"[7] and Aitken castigated the Minister for "far from being strict in his operational control of immigration and being "positively permissive".

It was this "ministerial permissiveness which had sown the seeds for the seething public discontent with immigration policy which has now erupted."[8]

But the Tory Party had its moments of contradictions, as Paul Foot illustrates.[9] Patrick Wall, MP for Halternprice, was a signatory to the Conservative Political Centre Report, Wind of Change, 1960, which contained this sentence:–

"There is enough experience in the Commonwealth to prove that harmony between races on a basis of partnership is a practical policy. We believe the mingling of culture leads to a richer and better society."

In 1965, however, while addressing the Conservative Central Council he said:–

"We must for the moment reject the multiracial state, not because we are superior to our Commonwealth partners but because we want to maintain the kind of Britain we know and love."

The Liberal Party, so far the least likely of the main parties to form a Government, have kept a steady position on race and immigration. David Steel's summary of the issues in 1969 is important:–

"While the human and social problems of immigration fall directly on certain parts of the country, it is a national problem. One of the disservices the Right Honourable Member for Wolverhampton SW has done has been not merely to exacerbate racial feeling in areas where there is a large immigrant population but to create fantasies and fears in parts of the country where there are no immigrants . . . . . If we condone white racialism in this country, we are encouraging Black, brown and yellow racialists in other countries to adopt the same logic and follow the same line of argument with regard to our fellow citizens elsewhere."[10]

The long standing right which colonial peoples had of free entry into Britain was enshrined in the 1948 Nationality Act which retained that right for such peoples who on independence decided to remain within the British Commonwealth of Nations. Indeed Britain was said to be dismantling an Empire and creating a Commonwealth. The Empire loyalists were quite happy to see the uppity Blacks who were calling for their independence swim or sink as best they could; while the industries were anxious to preserve both their source of raw material and access to a ready pool of unskilled and semi-skilled labour.

The immigrant labour force when it came settled in close proximity to the places of work. Since these were largely in the main urban areas characterised by old Victorian factories surrounded by areas of developing physical and social disintegration it is little surprise that as more and more Black immigrants went into those areas to live that dormant prejudices started to awaken and gave rise to open hostility.

Although the best analysis on this issue remains Paul Foot's *Immigration and Race in British Politics*, it is important to note that traditionally the Labour Party has always held the industrial conurbations. So that the Blacks settled for the most part in Labour-controlled areas. Besides they were largely working-class people and therefore the natural allies for the Labour Party; but their presence served Conservative Party interests.

Throughout the period 1951-1964, the Conservative Party was in power. The Conservative Government could thereby ignore the social consequences of Black immigration and leave those Labour-controlled local authorities to cope with it in whatever way they could and face the tensions of an already deprived white electorate. Thus it was that Labour councillors and MPs representing inner urban areas who were most vociferous in cataloguing every immigrant ill along with the Tory right wing composed of a strange mixture of the Empire loyalists and neo-fascists.

Britain's attempt to join the European Common Market created a situation that was later to bring the entire issue to a head. Her would-be European partners wanted to know whether Britain was joining with 55 millions or 805 millions. In other words was it the United Kingdom (England, Scotland, Wales and Northern Ireland) that was joining the EEC or was it the entire British Commonwealth. If it was the latter, then the answer would certainly be 'No'; if it was the former then modifications to the unfettered rights of entry granted under the 1948 Nationality Act would be needed.

The author is convinced that this requirement on the part of

Britain's would-be European partners did more than any other thing to open the gates of Britain's present racial situation. The first price of acceptance into Europe was the erosion of Black rights. It was a price the nation showed itself willing to pay. The introduction of immigration control on a *de facto* basis of colour provided a framework within which other forms of racial discrimination could strive. As successive government ministers sought to justify the policy, the seeds of public discontent with immigration policy were not only sown but grew into full grown trees ladened with the fruit of racialism.

Against this, the three mainstream political parties (Labour, Tory and Liberal) developed an all-party consensus that good race relations in Britain were dependent upon a limit on the number of Black immigrants who were let into the country. They even convinced themselves that strict immigration control was as much in the interest of the Black minorities as it was of the white majority.

All three of the major political parties also subscribed to a distinction between racial discrimination and racial disadvantage. In the debate on the Race Relations Bill in March 1976, here is how they put it:–

". . . a wide range of administrative and voluntary measures is needed in order to give practical effect to the objectives of the law. These measures are needed not only to combat discrimination and encourage equal opportunity but also to tackle what has come to be known as racial disadvantage."[11]
(Merlyn Rees – Labour)

". . . the other hazard, which is much more intractable and in my submission much more pervasive, is inescapable discrimination based upon disadvantage."[12]
(M. Alison – Tory)

"Anti-discrimination laws in themselves are not enough. Action must be taken to combat the disadvantages experienced by many people in minority communities – real disadvantages, not merely discrimination."[13]
(Alan Beith – Liberal)

It is easy to see how none of the major political parties understood the extent to which racial prejudice was creeping into immigration control policy and even when they did, they did not have the political will to deal with it as will be shown later when we discuss immigration and nationality in greater detail. The apparent exemplary record on race relations held by the Liberal Party nationally may in a large measure be due to the fact that they were never during this period in serious contention for forming the Government. Their position was never therefore really tested.

THE ULTRA RIGHT WING ANTI-IMMIGRANT PARTIES

A variety of right-wing racialists of "nationalist" political parties have developed in Britain since the end of World War II. Rose and others have argued that they have depended on the provocation of violent clashes and court cases for attention. Rose et al, however, contend that extremist groups, like the Birmingham Immigration Control Association, which were not political parties, but were formed specifically to campaign on anti-immigration platforms were more effective in influencing public opinion, and cite Paul Foot's study of the Smethwick campaign won by Peter Griffiths in 1964 in support of this view.[14]

While none of them has ever approached sufficient strength to gain power they have at various times exercised a sort of influence upon the major political parties – pushing them further and further to the right in their quest for the popular vote. They are conscious that they are appealing to the basest elements in human nature but do so unashamedly and with single-minded commitment. They maintain a rigid discipline and spend considerable time in the indoctrination of their members.

Having succeeded in pushing the Tory Government into introducing more stringent anti-immigrant legislation in 1971, the ultra right wing groups spearheaded by the National Front were still dissatisfied because the legislation fell short of a commitment to mass repatriation of Blacks. They embarked on a major recruitment campaign, gathering both the anti-Black voters and a section of the anti-Common Market elements of both parties.

In the local authority elections of May, 1974, the National Front entered over 1,000 candidates and not only did they stage a number of vital wins, but pushed Labour and Conservative candidates into third place in a number of places. They followed this electoral success up by fielding 90 candidates in the General Election in October of the same year. They became the fourth largest party contesting the election and although they lost their deposit in almost all cases, they did get an average of 3 per cent of the vote and did significantly well in areas where they were fighting elections for the first time, many of which did not have any sizeable numbers of Black residents.

Its manifesto, *For a New Britain*, contained a wide range of policies including the restoration of the death penalty, and the weeding out of the "great numbers of young people who go to University for entirely frivolous reasons." On immigration, it called for a total ban of further non-white immigration and a phased repatriation for all coloured immigrants and their descendants already here. While claiming that the programme would be put into effect with the greatest possible humanity, admitted "but we do not suppose it can be effective without some hardship to a portion of the people."[15]

A fuller discussion of the role of the Black vote in the election in 1974 follows later, but the loss of the anti-immigrant vote seriously damaged the fortunes of the Tory Party in the national elections. This explains in part the behaviour of both major parties in the 1979 General Elections on matters of race. The Labour Party tried to avoid annoying the anti-immigrant vote in its own midst, while the Tory Party actively, and with a measure of success, set out not only to keep their own anti-immigrant vote but also to capture a portion of the ultra-right wing vote.

The Economist of June 2, 1979, commenting on the results of the May 1979 General Election observed: "the issue of race caused a swing to the Conservatives of no more than 0.75 per cent, which is considerably less than the foreign press in particular have suggested. We find that without this support, the Conservatives would have won 16 fewer seats from Labour, leaving the Tories with a total of merely 323 seats."[16] That is to say that some National Front support shifted to the Tories and thus boosted their majority.

While many anti-racist groups saw the smaller National Front vote in the 1979 election compared with their vote in 1974 as something of a success for their campaigns during the intervening years, a more realistic analysis of what happened would be that the switch of the Tory Party to more openly anti-immigrant policies pulled back that vote into mainstream party voting and so cut down the size of the symbolic protest fringe vote.

IMMIGRATION CONTROL and NATIONALITY

I have already pointed to the pressures leading to the post-war wave of Black immigration into Britain and how the political forces gathered to demand some form of immigration control.

Part II of *Colour and Citizenship*, is a full discussion of coloured immigration to Britain.[17] Not only does it describe the countries from which the immigrants came, but also how immigration developed followed by the first efforts at control. The immigration control lobby had been active since the early 1950s but gathered

93

momentum after the race riots of 1958 and the restrictions surrounding entry into the Common Market. Ian Macleod lost the battle inside the Tory Party and the 1961 Commonwealth Immigration Act was introduced.

I support Cris Mullard's contention that white extremists saw the Act as a vindication of their position and a stimulus to their campaign to "keep Britain white". It was a first step upon which they could build. It had introduced the theory of an acceptable number of Blacks beyond which the social health of the nation would be in question. The Labour Party had argued that even if the Act was not *de jure* racialist it was certainly so in a *de facto* sense; and pledged themselves to repeal it, if and when they came to power.

The Act endowed immigration officers with wide powers of refusal backed up by substantial powers of detention and examination. They could submit individuals seeking entrance to the country to both medical and physical examination and demand all kinds of documentary evidence.

Entry was restricted to 30,000 and three categories of employment vouchers were introduced. Category A for professionally qualified, Category B for skilled workers, and Category C for unskilled workers. Students accepted to study at recognised institutions and persons who could prove that they could support themselves without seeking employment were allowed free entry.[18] So too were the dependants of those already resident in the United Kingdom.

Having decided on a process of Immigration Control, the Government had to meet four objectives in setting the limits of control. It had to satisfy the six countries of the EEC, pacify the liberal elements within the Party that it was not embarking on a racially discriminatory road, convince the right wing of the Party and the anti-immigrant lobby outside that it was taking effective action to halt the progress towards a multi-racial society; and reassure the Black states of the Commonwealth that its actions did not amount to abandonment. It was wholly successful in none of these.

It was denied entry into the Common Market and so for the time being in-so-far as the EEC was concerned the issue was irrelevant. The limit of 30,000 with its three categories of employment vouchers left the liberal lobby worried that the Government would not for long be able to defend it and that under pressure the limit would progressively be lowered. The right wing lobby condemned the limit as being too high and committed itself to bring it down. Whatever the Black states of the Commonwealth said publicly they realised that the "Mother Country" was involved in an act of economic separation, and that the offer of political independence to them was linked up with Britain's determination to stake her destiny with white Europe.

When Labour came to power foilowing the election in 1964, far from meeting their pledge to repeal the 1962 Commonwealth Immigrants Act, they proceeded to strengthen and tighten its provisions.

Labour's narrow victory had been due to the strength of support it had received from the Black community; but the evidence of the strength of the anti-immigrant vote had also been present. Patrick Gordon Walker, Labour's Shadow Foreign Secretary, and a well known and respected politician, lost his seat to a newcomer to national politics, Peter Griffiths, who fought a vicious anti-immigrant campaign. Labour was shocked that traditional Labour voters would respond so readily to the base coinage of racialism and decided to appease the anti-immigrant lobby.

U-turns are not unknown in politics, but what shattered the confidence of many Black voters was to hear Sir Frank Soskice, the Home Secretary, assert that the Labour Party had always been in favour of immigration control. The new Government was under three sources of pressure to reduce the number of Black people coming into the country. There were those who just wanted Black immigration stopped. Those who focussed their attack on illegal entrants and called for a tightening of rules and procedures and those representing local authorities in whose areas the immigrants had settled who argued that they could no longer cope with the new arrivals.

The Government responded in August, 1965, by cutting the number of entry vouchers from 30,000 to 8,500 a year, of this new number 1,000 were reserved for Maltese. But it also put an end to category C vouchers which were used by unskilled workers. In addition it greatly strengthened the powers of immigration officers. This action on the part of the Labour Party in betraying the loyalty of their Black voters so undermined their confidence in the democratic process that it took a decade before Black people returned to the polls in any great numbers.

In 1968, the anti-immigration lobby received its most valued prize. The Right Honourable Enoch Powell MP, for Wolverhampton SW, a Greek scholar of the classical tradition and perhaps the best Parliamentary orator of his generation, decided to throw his immense personal prestige and parliamentary skill behind the campaign being waged by the anti-immigration lobby, but without joining the lobby itself. He was himself Member of Parliament for an area having to cope with the flow of immigration and this added credibility to what he was saying.

Besides, good performer as he was, the media loved him and he in turn loved them. This brought Powell and what he had to say into every living room on TV, radio and on the front pages of newspapers delivered to the breakfast table. No other single person has had so great an impact on the race scene in Britain over the past twenty years.

On Friday, February 9, 1968, Enoch Powell addressed the Annual Dinner of the Walsall South Conservative Association. Inter alia he said:–

"There is a sense of hopelessness and helplessness which comes over persons who are trapped or imprisoned, when all their efforts to attract attention and assistance brings no response. This is the kind of feeling which you in Walsall and we in Wolverhampton are experiencing in the case of the continued flow of immigration into our towns . . . Recently those of us who live in the Midlands and in other areas directly affected have been startled to learn that a provision in the Kenya Independence Act and similar British legislation has the unexpected effect that some 200,000 Indians in Kenya alone have become literally indistinguishable from the people of the United Kingdom, so that they have an absolute right of entry to this country."[19]

This speech had the effect of panicking the Labour Government. The bandwagons of the immigration control lobby were once more on the run. This time they succeeded in pushing the Government into passing the 1968 Commonwealth Immigrants Act. The possession of a British passport no longer conferred freedom of entry without let or hinderance to its legal holder. It all depended on who the legal holder was. The Act, besides limiting the rights of certain British passport holders, also further limited the right of dependants by invoking a sole responsibility condition. The Labour Government rushed through the Bill in less than a week. They had the support of the Tory Front Bench, but were opposed by the Liberal Party, fifteen Tory MPs and some 35 Labour MPs. From outside the House the measure was opposed by both the Archbishop of Canterbury, then chairman of the National Committee for Commonwealth Immigrants, and Mark Bonham-Carter, chairman of the Race Relations Board.[20]

Its main purpose was to limit the absolute right of entry which until now the holding of a British passport had ensured, and was particularly aimed at Asians in East Africa, who, on British advice, had opted for the retention of British nationality as opposed to that of the East African State in which they resided. But the Act also seriously affected rights enjoyed by Caribbean peoples through introducing the concept of sole responsbility as a condition for being able to gain an entry certificate for a dependant resident in the West Indies. Successive tribunals have ruled that it is not legally possible to be solely responsible for a dependant in the West Indies if one is normally resident in England.

In pushing through the legislation in just one week, the Government ignored the advice of the Race Relations bodies it had itself set up and their chairman: – the Archbishop of Canterbury of the National Committee for Commonwealth Immigrants, and Mark Bonham-Carter of the Race Relations Board – expressed regret at the Government's failure to consult on the issue. Certainly the position whereby the value of a passport was determined by the holder and not the issuing Government, or that Government would issue passports of differing status and value is not a healthy one. Yet this was precisely the result of the 1968 Immigration Act and the rules that followed it.

More important still is the fact that the intervention of Enoch Powell into the race relations debate was centred on the concept of incompatible numbers. It is a tragedy that the entire race relations lobby joined the debate on those terms. Their failure to appreciate that the real debate ought to have been about racism and not about numbers has lost the black cause nearly a decade of very valuable time.

In 1971, the Tory Government introduced the concept of "patriality" in yet another Immigration Act, and promised a new Nationality Act. Before they could do anything about it they went out of power, but the Labour Party, who regained power as a minority Government, although publishing a Green Paper (Consultative Document) on nationality never took it any further. The Green Paper (Prov) tended to support an acceptance of the principle of patriality enshrined in the 1971 Immigration Act. It would have sought to confer British citizenship on patrials and a few others while for almost all non-patrials there would be a status of British Overseas Citizenship. The former would carry rights of entry and abode, the latter would not.

As soon as the Tories returned to power in May 1979 they turned their attention to tightening the rules governing entry. It is important to bear in mind that the Tories owed much to the anti-immigrant vote for the strength of their position in the present Parliament. The fact that in so doing they were able to find a formula for exempting most white women from the rules depriving women of the right to bring their husbands and fiances into the country established beyond doubt the racist nature of the rules.

But even the rules governing the rights of men to bring their wives and fiancees in are not free from prejudice. It was discovered in early 1980 that many Black women were subject to virginity tests before entry clearance was ganted. This discovery of the further zeal with which immigration control rules are pursued caused some embarassment not only to the Government but also to David Lane, then chairman of the Commission for Racial Equality who was Under-Secretary of State at the Home Office in 1971, at the time when the virginity tests were first introduced. He has denied knowledge of it.

It is clear that much of the confusion over immigration rules in the aftermath of the 1968 Immigration Act sprang from the Nationality provisions of the Nationality Act 1948. Successive governments have therefore been committed to changing the Nationality law. In November, 1979, Ann Dummett wrote:–

"Within the next two years, there will almost certainly be a new British Nationality Act. It will contain a completely new definition of what it means to be British; and the legal status of most of the 55 million people in Britain and millions outside it will change . . . . Some minorities may fear too much: the public at large certainly is not fearful enough of what a new Nationality Act could do . . . There is a strong possibility that the status of "British Subject" will be abolished or greatly modified and it is to that status that the rights of all of us to vote, stand for election, and work in the public service are attached.

"Other rights and duties go with it . . . . There are two main questions facing the Government now. What status should it give to all the people in the world who are at present British in the sense of being eligible for British passports? And what to do about the concept of the subject, hitherto fundamental to our law?."

"The options open to it are in fact very wide, but the Government is apparently approaching the problem with three major policy assumptions in mind which are going to make satisfactory solutions difficult. First, that there should be in future

a citizenship of the United Kingdom alone, separate from the colonies. Second, that the new laws most important effect will be to "remove some of the possible sources of future immigration" (i.e. non-white immigration). Third, that the rules on acquiring British nationality should be restrictively, not expansively drawn."[21]

Ann Dummett, in analysing the position of the three main parties, notes that the Liberal Party Working Group had suggested retaining a united citizenship with the colonies until the last of them had become independent. The Conservative Lawyers' Working Group recommended in 1975, that each colony should have its own citizenship in future, and the Labour Government's Green Paper in 1977, suggested a single British Overseas Citizenship for the colonies, non-patrials like the East African British Asians who hold British passports but have no colony to belong to, and for British Protected Persons.

The Green Paper plan was based broadly on the acceptance of the patriality concept of the 1971 Immigration Act. It proposed British citizenship for patrials and a very few others with rights of entry to the United Kingdom and British Overseas Citizenship for almost all non-patrials with no such rights. Neither the Green Paper nor the Conservative Lawyers Working Party go beyond the discussion of right of entry and so Ann Dummett concludes that "we seem likely to get a crippled form of nationality defined in immigration terms alone", and that worse, since immigration control if effectively racial, we may well get a racial nationality bill.[22]

The Government's majority however, did allow them to introduce legislation in the sure knowledge that they had the votes in both Houses of Parliament to see it through. It replaced the longstanding and worldwide citizenship of the United Kingdom and Colonies which was common to all British citizens, with a three-tier system of citizenship:–

(a) British citizenship for people "closely connected with the UK"
(b) Citizenship of the British Dependent Territories for people connected with dependencies; and
(c) British Overseas Citizenship for the remaining citizens of the United Kingdom and Colonies.

This principle of three-tier citizenship, rather than one common citizenship has aroused considerable hostility as indeed much of the Government's intentions. The Prime Minister, Mrs Margaret Thatcher, paid a visit to India during the passage of the Bill through Parliament and the Indian press conveyed in no uncertain terms the anxieties of the people of the Indian sub-continent. On her return to England, she gave an interview on a weekly BBC Television programme for Asian viewers in a bold attempt to assuage their fears. It was not lost on the West Indian community that she made no similar attempt to deal with their anxieties over the Bill.

The Bill also attracted considerable opposition from the official spokesmen of the Labour Party who pledged themselves to repeal it when next they came to power. It is not surprising that the reaction amongst a large section of the Black community was one of *deja vu*. In order to ensure its passage, it was necessary for the Government to impose a guillotine on the Committee Stage of the Bill. Despite strong opposition in the House of Lords by the Church of England bishops, who repeated the concerns of the Churches, the Government, as expected, won the day.

INSTITUTIONS
We have observed that when Labour came to power in 1964, the Government tightened the rules and regulations governing the functioning of the 1962 Commonwealth Immigrants Act which it had promised to repeal while in opposition. As a sop to the Blacks who were bitterly disappointed by this action, the Government set up the National Committee for Commonwealth Immigrants (NCCI) whose function was to inform and educate public opinion and work towards creating a favourable climate in which integration could take place. It also had the task of encouraging the development of local groups, known as liaison committees, who would seek to remove areas of local tension and promote racial harmony.

As further evidence of the Government's good intentions it steered through Parliament the first Race Relations Act in 1965. The Act set up the Race Relations Board (RRB) and made a limited number of acts of racial discrimination unlawful. The Board had the duty to investigate all complaints brought to it and form an opinion as to whether or not discrimination had taken place. Where the Board formed such an opinion it would seek to conciliate and only where conciliation failed would court action be taken.

It is clear that had the Government not felt obliged to do something to meet the feelings of deep resentment by Blacks at its failure to repeal the 1962 Immigration Act, that these two institutions might never have come into being. Mullard sums up the position in relation to the White Paper which set up the NCCI in these terms:–

"The core of the Government's case was that race relations could be improved only if there were effective immigration controls. Unaware of the implicit contradiction, the Government outlined a programme for racial harmony. On the one hand politicians propounded that racial harmony was dependent on immigration control, on the other that harmony was dependent on "integrating" Black immigrants into the "host" community."

"If you accept that Britain was already a racist country, then restrictions on entry could hardy erase racism. Similarly, "integration" programmes in a racist society will not have the slightest beneficial effect – if anything, they produce more hostility."

"The emphasis of the NCCI further reflected the Government's confusion. Its very title – The National Committee for Commonwealth Immigrants – and the choice of Chairman, the present Archbishop of Canterbury, exemplified the Government's view that race relations had more in common with Christianity and social work than with politics."[23]

The Government's case was centred on the mistaken conviction that race relations could only be improved in the presence of an effective battery of immigration controls. Indeed the Government appeared to have accepted a correlation between the number of Blacks in the society and the prospects of racial harmony. Successive Governments fail to appreciate the inherent contradiction in its strategy, but also that its perception of the nature of race relations was brought into question.

The concept that too many Blacks were a danger to racial harmony and that as a consequence rigid immigration controls, regardless of the social consequences to Blacks and their families, were essential in the interests of the country only stimulated the numbers game and besides awakening racial prejudice in whites, it reinforced feelings of isolation, rejection and inferiority in Blacks. It has a totally negative effect on the process of integrating Blacks into white society. The Government fell into this dichotomy because it was unable to perceive, or accept it if it did perceive it, that the level of racism in the society was such that mere restriction on entry of Blacks could no longer suffice and that indeed any policy of restriction which it introduced would feed that climate of racism and increase demand and ultimately lead to an insatiable cry from the racists. Indeed, it is now a matter of record that the racists interpreted the Government's meagre efforts at an integration programme as sheer duplicity and humbug.

Considering the task of public education placed on the NCCI, its title National Committee for Commonwealth Immigrants was a misnomer and led to considerable confusion among Blacks and whites alike; and as Cris Mullard points out; choice of the Archbishop of Canterbury as its first chairman "exemplified the Government's view that race relations had more to do with Christianity and social work than with politics"

Be that as it may, the NCCI was to face an even greater problem than that of Government's indifference to its views. Barely six months after coming into being, the NCCI was so impressed by the strength of feeling up and down the country as a result of the Government's immigration policies and the extent to which those feelings were frustrating its work that not only did it feel impelled to say so in its first six monthly report, but, in addition, sent off a deputation to see the Prime Minister to advise him of the wide range of people and organisations who had objections to the size and nature of the controls. Not a single concession was made. The fact that the NCCI had a meagre grant of £50,000 to do a national public relations job for the Government in an area of social policy as sensitive as race relations would have been compensated for if only the Government had given asmuch as a pretence of having listened to what it had to say.

Rose et al[24] have contended that having created the NCCI the Government proceeded to abdicate its responsibility for the race relations climate. It now had an effective buffer mechanism. Whether it was challenged on the inadequacy of its public education programme on race relations, or the lack of consistent guide-lines for local and national policies towards Blacks, or on the loss of Black confidence, it would point to the NCCI's role in these matters. If failure there was, then it was due to the NCCI.

The major success of the NCCI, due largely to its energetic General Secretary, Nadine Peppard, was the creation of local voluntary committees (later to become Community Relations Councils) in each of the urban centres with a substantial number of Blacks. Her enthusiasm for these and her general commitment to better welfare conditions for Blacks surmounted the problems of both the inconsistency of the Government's policies and the inadequacy of funding.

But these were to suffer the same malaise as their parent body arising from a lack of clarity of role. There were broad based multi-racial organisations comprised of representatives of various organisations in the towns they served. Built for consensus there was constant tension between the desires of those who wanted to press the case on behalf of Blacks with vigour and those who were ever anxious to retain the confidence of the local authority. Like Central Government, many local authorities saw in the local liaison committee a convenient buffer and an alibi for their continued neglect of Black needs. Whether or not, therefore, one accepts Paul Foot's three conclusions[25] that the liaison committees through associating the three main political parties with multi-racialism lessened the possibility of official candidates openly canvassing for the racist vote; that through helping Blacks with simple matters of welfare and the like they made anti-immigrant propaganda less acceptable and that many of them provided an effective counter-weight to the propaganda of Fascists and anti-immigrant organisations, it must be said that they lacked the conceptual basis for an attack on institutionalised racism and the political punch to ensure fundamental change in service delivery.

John Rex, a member of the NCCI's Housing Panel, in his critique of the NCCI offers the opinion that its failure rests in a basic ambiguity of role and argues that the NCCI never resolved the division between its social work function and its political role. Additionally, it was beset by weakness in its bureaucratic machinery. The cumulative effect was an ineffective organisation.[26]

Dipak Nandy, himself an NCCI member, spoke of it as being "paralysed with fear, so that it could move neither to the right nor the left".[27]

But this political impotence was inescapable given the fact that the organisation had no statutory powers and the task the Government wanted done was not one of social change but that of allaying fears among Black and white citizens alike through an avoidance of the issues of racism.

The Government had always argued that one of the chief tasks of the NCCI was to advise the Government on all matters relating to race relations and immigration. That being the case it was a measure of the Government's sincerity and commitment to good race relations that it did not consult the NCCI when it was about to rush through the 1968 Commonwealth Immigrants Act. So disgusted were a number of people by the contempt the Government had shown for the NCCI that they withdrew from the Committee and its panels. Others resigned from the local committees. For many, this was the final indignity. One former member of the NCCI said –

"I don't think the Government wanted to seek our advice, as knowing we'd disagree with the proposals it felt it safer to introduce them quicker. They never paid much attention to what we said anyway. Now and again, I wondered if we were serving any purpose other than keeping an eye on developments."[28]

The Race Relations Board on the other hand was a statutory body set up under Act of Parliament in 1965. The Government's approach to Black misgivings over the immigration issue was to say that it was doing all it could to ensure that those who were here were being treated kindly and made to feel welcome, hence the NCCI and the local liaison committees and finally, the Race Relations Board. It is certainly an indication of Government's assessment of Black aspirations that the 1965 Race Relations Act restricted itself to making unlawful discrimination in "public places" and then went on to exempt almost as many places as it covered. Not only were the enforcement procedures weak but the processes used to arrive at decisions were long and tedious. None of the serious areas of genuine concern – discrimination in housing, jobs, education, insurance, finance services – was included in the Act.

Two independent pieces of research were commissioned in 1966. Professor Street was asked to study race laws and procedures in other countries and make recommendations, and the Political and Economic Planning team were asked to examine the extent of racial discrimination. The Race Relations Board, to its credit, realised the limitations of the scope within which it functioned and supported the commissioning of these two independent pieces of research. Both the Street Report and the Political and Economic Planning Report stressed the substantial nature of racial discrimination in British society and identified the fields of employment, housing and education as areas needing urgent attention.

One still questions the wisdom of the Street Report that the "conciliation" principle should be retained since this was held to be less likely to antagonise white opinion than if one sought a punitive remedy.

The PEP Report in particular showed conclusively that racial minority groups faced a very substantial amount of unfair discrimination when seeking jobs and housing, and in a number of other fields as well. It revealed that the major component in the discrimination was colour.

The Report summed up the situation this way –

"It is moreover impossible to escape the conclusion that the more different a person is in his physical characteristics, in his features, in the texture of his hair and in the colour of his skin, the more discrimination he will face."[29]

Unwittingly by implication, what the Street Report was suggesting was that the level of racial prejudice in the society was so high that the risk of white backlash resulting from the punishment of white people who discriminated against Black people was so great as to make the concept of punishment counterproductive. Invoking the principle of government by consent, the Government argued that it would be unwise to antagonise white opinion since the success of the legislation depended upon their co-operation. It brought in a new 1968 Race Relations Act, extended the scope of discriminatory acts to include employment, housing, education and services. It also gave the Race Relations Board new powers to investigate without having to wait to be approached by an individual complainant where it had reason to believe discriminatory acts were taking place. It however retained the "conciliation" principle.

At the same time the Government replaced the NCCI with a statutory body known as the Community Relations Commission. It continued the same functions of the NCCI – information and public education, advice to Government and its other agencies, and support for local voluntary race relations work. While nothing was done to clarify the ambiguities of role which plagued the NCCI, the new arrangement made the body more accountable to Government and the new name further blurred the issues.

The Act made no attempt to define what was meant by good harmonious community relations and when the local liaison committees rushed to rename themselves community relations councils the trend away from fighting racism took on a gallop.

With the question of its political role unresolved and with its major objective "good harmonious community relations" undefined, the organisation continued to be torn by differing philosophical loyalties. Could it, indeed should it, campaign militantly for Black rights or should it work quietly for harmony? In the long run endeavouring to please all, it succeeded in satisfying none. Government continued to take little notice of it but sheltered behind its presence whenever a crisis in race relations had to be faced.

But if the Community Relations Commission was having difficulty in coming to terms with its own role, it began to have even greater difficulty with the local community relations councls who were particularly jealous of their independence as local voluntary organisations. Many of them saw the replacing of the NCCI by the statutory CRC as a move on the part of Government to more firmly control the central body and through it the criticism of the Government's race relations policy that was coming up from the grassroots.

Hill and Issacharoff, in their study of community relations councils, conclude:–

"The community relations committee has the worst of all possible situations. It is a voluntary organisation, yet cannot use all the pressure group tactics of public sponsored criticism because it is a quasi-statutory body dependent on the support of a Government-created national agency. At the same time, it has no statutory powers of its own and cannot compel a local authority to co-operate or even, in some cases, acknowledge its existence."

. . . *"The community relations officer's power in the public and private spheres depends upon the support of Central Government. Their support from local authorities is rarely an asset and often a liability, and their support from the non-official members of their committees largely irrelevant. They could therefore be expected to operate much more effectively without the constraints imposed by the existing local committee structure. The local immigrant and pro-immigrant organisations would equally operate better as independent pressure groups outside the strictures imposed by a consensual committee."*

. . . *"Voluntary organisations at present are not democratic or representative in any true sense. It seems spurious to justify control of community relations committees over professional staff in terms of "democracy" or "community" control."*[30]

One further problem rested in the fact that local immigrant and pro-immigrant groups had too large an expectation of them and local authorities following in the footsteps of Central Government paid little or no attention to the suggestions for policy change made by them.

The Barker typology[31] of local community relations councils is helpful in that it is not only a statement of style but also an expression of the level of resolution of the inherent conflicts and a measure of the maturity of the organisation in facing up to the issues of racial discrimination. The shelter-type was the basic pseudo-welfare organisation avoiding any political issues while assisting immigrants with such problems as language interpretation, information on available services and general social agencies. The bridge-type acted more as a facilitator, providing a meeting place or forum for community groups from the Black communities and others to meet for mutual discussion of issues. The platform-type accepted the full responsibility of a campaigning organisation, drawing public attention to the many problems resulting from racial discrimination and inner city deprivation.

If the Community Relations Commission (CRC) and the local community relations councils associated with it suffered from ambiguities of role, the Race Relations Board (RRB) had no such handicap. At least it had a clear mandate. Like the CRC its members were appointed by the Home Secretary. He ensured that there were Black members on the Board but these were neither in large enough numbers or of the temperament to stamp their image or that of the Black community on the body. Tied to the "conciliation" principle and buttressed by an unimaginative bureaucracy, all initiatives and purpose was stifled and staff morale was low. The task of ferreting out and destroying racial discrimination rather than becoming a vigorous and challenging pursuit got relegated into a staid moribund characterless exercise. What is more, the RRB, despite its mandate to flight racial discrimination found difficulty for a long time in taking on Black staff except in the lowliest of positions and those it took on found it near impossible to gain promotion.

Two quotes from conciliation officers at the Board would illustrate the mood inside that organisation.[32]

> "One of the most disappointing aspects of the Board seems to be that, to all intents and purposes, those of us on the staff were recruited originally for showing a certain amount of initiative and for caring, in a positive sense, about the value of the work we try to do, and yet, once employed, we seem to be stifled and discouraged from ever using our initiative and enthusiasm. None of us joined the staff because we longed for a bureaucratic life surrounded by endless memoranda, but because we were excited about the job there is to do in race relations."

and another said –

> "It is common knowledge that we are not at all happy in our working but I don't think many people grasp the extent of the trouble. Let me specify. Leaving aside junior staff too numerous to mention, the following senior staff have left the Board . . . in my time: two Secretaries to the Board, one Principal Conciliation Officer, two Principal Information Officers, two Information

Officers, ten Conciliation Officers and one Assistant Conciliation Officer. When you remember that the total conciliation staff has never exceeded twenty-four, this is quite a record. Add the fact that no coloured employee of the Board has ever been promoted, and that there has never been a coloured person on the Board's headquarters staff. . ."

While as a consequence of the statutory powers of the 1968 Race Relations Act the white establishment was able to tighten its grasp on the race relations bureaucracy. Blacks who had entered the service of the local community relations councils were using that platform to articulate Black needs and, aided by the vagueness of role definition and tradition of local autonomy for voluntary groups, worked out a strategy for mounting sorties on various aspects of Government policy while demanding greater democratisation of the CRC and its response to community needs.

Mark Bonham-Carter, who as chairman of the RRB had been credited with the high esteem and firm position held by that body, was brought to the CRC in 1971 with the major task of bringing local work under control and centralising the employment of officers and apparently, to halt the advance being made by Blacks into the race relations bureaucracy. The local committees responded by forming their own association, the National Association of Community Relations Councils (NACRC) and jointly with the officers union (ASTMS) successfully resisted the take over bid.

However, for a time the decline of Black influence was speeded up. Few analysts challenge Mullard's observation that the appointment of white officers at all levels coupled with the drop in Black appointments cast serious doubts on the Commission's multi-racial concept.[33]

In 1973, three Black community relations officers felt that unless the emasculation of the Black influence was stopped then it would not be long before the whole race relations system would be a total irrelevance to the Black community. It was nonsense for white CRC officials to be preaching the virtues of having Blacks in decision-making and policy-making positions when their own organisation could be found wanting. The three Black officers reported the Community Relations Commission and its chairman, Mark Bonham-Carter, to the Race Relations Board and sought an investigation of the recruitment and promotion procedures of the Commission. Both bodies became aware that Blacks were no longer prepared to be left out of the decision-making corridors

108

of the race relations bureaucracy and they as well as their Government masters reacted in typical fashion. Although the CRC made the greater response, both bodies took on a number of Blacks and promoted a few others, this was to be short-lived, as we shall see.

The Government soon announced that it would be changing some of the rules of the game. It would merge the CRC and the RRB into one body in a marriage of convenience. The new body became known as the Commission for Racial Equality. In order to allow the white establishment to weed out Black militants the Home Secretary gave the chairman designate, David Lane, the right not to employ all the staff of the CRC and the RRB. The only two he failed to offer jobs were the two senior officers at the CRC who were most in contact with the local voluntary organisations and the Black communities. The Black communities made it clear that they would see it as an act of unwarranted hostility if the two did not get their jobs back and would act accordingly. As a result, David Lane offered them jobs but outside of the functional policy and decision-making framework.

In theory the Commission for Racial Equality, created under the 1976 Race Relations Act, should have been a much stronger body. It might have been had its planners not been so obsessed with the emasculation of Black influence. At least the name made it quite clear what the organisation's business was about. It was in the business of racial equality. Its first duty was working towards the elimination of racial discrimination. Its second was promoting equality of opportunity and good relations between persons of different racial groups. The Act removed the buffer role of the RRB and gave direct access to Industrial Tribunals in the case of employment cases and the County Court in all other cases to the victims of discrimination. It gave the Commission wide powers of strategic investigation into institutional racism armed with powers to sub-poena and the quasi-judicial power to issue non-discriminatory notices enforceable by the courts. In addition it created a new area of discrimination, the indirect discriminatory act. In all an impressive battery of provisions but hardly of any benefit until used effectively.

Rather than grasp the opportunities provided by the new Act, Lane and his planners set about the deployment of staff in such a way as to revive all the old antagonisms both in respect of a white elitist control of the bureaucracy as well as the resurgence of a "softly-softly" approach to strategic investigations. After four years the organisation was still approaching its strategic investigations with, on the one hand a lack of urgency and on the other a timidity born of uncertainty in a fickle political climate. It had been unable to overcome its legacy of self-destroying elements.

The organisation was receiving a bad press, and two letters which appeared in the *New Statesman* following an article by Anna Coote and Mike Phillips illustrated the cul-de-sac into which Lane had led it and that the new organisation, two years after its inception on 13 June 1977, was still suffering from the malaise of its predecessor bodies.

David Lane, chairman, Commission for Racial Equality, wrote:

"Your article "The Quango no Referr" (NS 13 July) was full of inaccuracies and gave a distorted picture of the CRE . . . As a Commission we are not in a state of perpetual tug-of-war as your article implied. At Commission meetings we thoroughly air any differences of opinion and almost invariably reach a consensus . . . As for the "tea party" principle, our job is both law enforcement and persuasion; we would be foolish if we concentrated wholly on coercion and neglected the scope for co-operation . . . There is no question of our wanting to hold back the self-help movement."[34]

Referring to the same article, Kate Francis, Executive Officer of the National Association of Community Relations Councils, wrote:–

"The CRE has enormous difficulty in, first deciding and secondly implementing any working policy outside the legislatively defined areas of conducting investigations and assisting complainants. The symptoms are obvious to those of us in regular contact: inability to make decisions, failure to respond to initiative, confusion and delay. it is tempting, and not entirely wrong, to interpret this as commitment to consensus and conspiracy to confuse. Sadly the truth usually lies closer to managerial cock-up allied to managerial indecision. It is one thing exhorting a well-oiled machine to change direction, it is quite another to exhort a jelly-fish that it is going roughly the right way to stop being a jelly-fish and start being something else. But that is what we have to do."[35]

Against this background David Lane in launching the Commission Plan 80 said that the Commission saw its role as that of an independent agency for change, an uncompromising advocate and campaigner for social justice.[36] But many of the Commission's friends agree that it is just this kind of lofty rhetoric which is unmatched by deeds that undermines the Commission's credibility in the eyes of the Black community. In the issues near and dear to the heart of the Black community, the SUS law, virginity testing and on immigration issues to mention a few, the Commission is never seen to be a leader, and as a follower is oftimes so far behind it cannot be seen at all. Indeed, when it does act it comes up against the formidable instruments of the bureaucracy for which it has not yet devised an adequate and appropriate response.

SOME OTHER STRATEGIES
It is worth noting three specific funding strategies which the Government employed in an attempt to buy the co-operation of those local authorities most affected by Black settlement. The first was given effect through Section 11 of the 1966 Local Government Act. Central Government contributed through this fund 75 per cent of expenditure on staff who became necessary because of services required as a consequence of the settlement of immigrants within the local authority's area. The immediate services to benefit were education and social services although some local authorities did extend their claim to other activities.

Central Government did nothing to monitor the fund and thus ensure that the service delivery to the Black community was in fact improved by the expenditure. It is a matter of serious complaint that a number of local authorities having played the numbers game and received staff resources then re-deployed them in other areas of need within the white sector. Because of this, Black confidence in local authority practice has been severely weakened.

The second programme was launched under the Local Government Grant (Social Need) Act 1969 and was known as the Urban Aid Programme. Unlike the Section 11 funding which met staffing needs only and was tied to the provision of services to Blacks, Urban Aid was linked to general social need and Black need was only one criterion. Besides Urban Aid was also intended to stimulate community based voluntary projects. Here again, Central Government would provide 75 per cent of the expenditure the other 25 per cent being supplied by the local authority.

However, two difficulties faced the Black community. In many ways the schemes which they were putting forward represented unorthodox answers to societal problems and local authority officials found difficulty in assessing their value and coupled with that the organisations invariably had no management track record. To safeguard themselves the bureaucrats imposed unacceptable conditions. The second difficulty lay in the fact that Central Government funding took on a "pump-priming" role and that at the end of the Central Government's funding period the project organisers would naturally be turning to the local authority for full support. In those circumstances the local authority were reluctant to support schemes which did not fall naturally into their own concepts of social planning. Because of this latter fact, some local authorities were reluctant to get involved. One policy maker has described it as "one huge con trick" and another as "the most half-witted system that can ever have been devised."[37]

Cross argues that the Urban Aid Programme is unique in that it is concerned with providing additional resources in urban areas which contain areas of social need for the carrying on of practical projects here and now rather than a research programme looking into the future. He adds that it is also unique in that it incorporates a policy of "positive discrimination" in favour of areas which have many of the core problems of urban deprivation and has made it possible for local authorities to make "some provision for particular categories of people within their areas who have special needs vis-a-vis others."[38]

The value of the Urban Aid Programme to the Black community was in the end small in real terms but it may well be that its importance lay in what Cross describes as the unique features of the programme in the provision of additional resources to meet social needs in urban areas of stress and the principal of "positive action" which it incorporates. perhaps it is this precedence that Blacks can best use in claiming funds for their special needs.

The third programme was in fact a re-vamping of the Urban Aid Programe. After a series of studies of inner city areas aimed at developing a corporate approach to the improvement of the environment, the Government finally launched a major Inner Cities programme. The vast majority of Blacks live in what is known as the Inner City areas. Despite this, the Inner Cities Programme has no specific racial dimension. In its concern with practical action in areas of urban deprivation, Cross says that Central Government has embraced a policy of strong discrimination legislation combined with a policy of general provision for all those who live in such areas irrespective of their racial, cultural and religious background. This has been done on the presumption that (*a*) a policy of general provision would benefit members of ethnic minority groups as well as members of the indigenous population; and, (*b*) it would contribute towards equality of treatment of all groups.[39]

The Secretary of State for the Environment supported this policy when he stated in *Race Relations and Housing:–*

> *"While immigrants and their families living in inner urban areas share the disadvantages of those areas with the very many others living there, they may have added difficulties of racial discrimination, of gaining access to information, of understanding housing law, procedures and practice."*[40]

Indeed, the report of the Central Policy Review Staff (SPRS) is very emphatic:–

> *"We are here (in the context of urban deprivation policies) concerned with poverty in a wider sense: the condition of people whose command over resources generally – income, educational and occupational skills, environment at home or at work, material possessions falls very seriously short of the average in the community. A 'poverty strategy' must be consistent with social policy towards the community as a whole."*[41]

The theory was that instead of spreading funds thinly, it would be better to concentrate on those Inner City areas where there was evidence of physical and social disintegration and mount large scale programmes there. The Government's mind was firmly set against any specific race relations component to the scheme relying only on the belief that since the majority of Blacks live in the Inner City areas, any improvements carried out through the Inner Cities Programme must benefit Blacks. This is typical of the ostrich attitude towards race and neither history nor current experience was on the side of Government. It was an act of misguided faith.

It could not be expected that local and Central Government officials who had neglected Black needs for over three decades would suddenly, because they had more funds, have a sudden attitudinal change to service delivery and resource allocation. Nor indeed could a weakly organised, disadvantaged and powerless minority, further handicapped by institutional discrimination be able to compete with equal opportunity for what was going.

LAW AND ORDER ISSUES

Two things have tended to keep alive the air of suspicion between the police and the Black community. The first is related to the

113

Government's immigration policy which has fed the feeling of rejection in the Black community and encouragement among white fascist elements. The police are viewed as the sharp-end of the enforcement of racist policies and the defenders and protectors of racists. These feelings get reinforced everytime the police are used in a raid of employers' premises or hostels or boarding houses during the early hours of the morning in search of illegal immigrants or when they turn out in large numbers to protect provocative National Front marches through predominantly Black areas.

Following the enactment of the 1971 Immigration Act, and an outburst of conflict with the police, the autumn issue of *Black Voice* carried this comment:–

"The racist pig police have embarked on more bold-face attacks on the Black community. We will not be fooled. These attacks are planned tactics, brought into being in order to create a suitable atmosphere, in which the Immigration Act can be easily enforced. These attacks are all part and parcel of the ruling class's general plan to curb any sign of visible resistance to creeping fascism by the working class."[42]

The second is related to police behaviour itself. The reports of police harassment of Blacks are legend. These stretch from simple abuse, through brutal assault, to death in police custody. The use of "SUS" powers which form part of the general complaint of harassment has emerged as the focal point of concern among the Black community.

The Government has now withdrawn the "SUS" powers and a new Criminal Attempt Act has come into force. It will take time to judge its effects. The 1971 Annual Report of the National Council of Civil Liberties boldly stated that it was clear from their files that the alleged harassment of immigrants far outweighed the proportion they represented in the country.[43]

Derek Humphrey, in his book *Police Power and Black People,* spends a chapter setting out the early stages of police community relations programmes,[44] and the author in an unpublished address to a conference of senior police officers in 1979 admitted that although of all the services the police had made the greatest effort in terms of in-service training and in community effort representing as they did the front line of the guardianship of racist society, they were still viewed very much with suspicion.[45] What is alarming is the fact that the police authorities having done more than any other statutory agency by way of in-service training

114

and community effort to try to break down the barriers of suspicion still find themselves at the butt of Black hostility with white society. It may well be that they waited too long before moving in the direction of recruitment and consequently have been fighting against too many odds. Recruitment will continue to be difficult **until the police can succeed in changing their repressive image.**

A frightening number of young Black people believe that it would be impossible for them to go into a police station alone without being beaten up by the police. The level of fear which they exhibit and the resentment and hostility which they harbour present problems not only for the police but for themselves. Indeed both Michael Banton[46] and John brown[47] assert that this level of tension in the relationship between the police and young Blacks gives rise to minor difficulties escalating into major instances of confrontation and consequent police action.

In 1978, the National Youth Bureau conducted a survey of the relationship between young people and the police. They found that Black youth especially of West Indian origin experienced far greater levels of fear, resentment and hostility in dealing with the police than their white counterparts. One youth worker reported that he did not think one could find 50 Black people in his area who would willing walk into a police station on their own. If they had to go, they always went as three or four, never as one person, because they were afraid.[48]

Remarking on how the courts are struck by the resentment which many young Blacks feel for the police, Donald Ford, chairman of Inner London Juvenile Magistrates, said he believed that the police reflected the broad spectrum of attitudes towards the coloured population. Their intervention was generally into situations of greatest stress and their appearance on the scene could be an additional stress factor. They could not opt out of those situations, even if they wished to, the anger, suspicion and resentment of the youngsters focussed on them for that reason.

Arguing further that society had failed to acknowledge or come to terms with the problem he said that they were busy discussing the preservation of their own cultural standard at a time when many of the youngsters were lost, and felt abandoned, in a desert between conflicting and contrasting cultures. There was still time to repair the damage brought about by their own pre-occupation, insensitivity and neglect, but that time was running out. If the effort was not made, there could be much more trouble in store in the future.[49]

Nothing more accurately illustrates his position as the way in which the Government rejected the recommendations of the Parliamentary Select Committee on Race Relations and Immigration that the Home Secretary should invite the Commission for Racial Equality to set up a working party on which representatives of both the Police and the West Indian community should be members. Not only did the Government decide that the working party was not the best way to proceed, but endorsed the continuing consultation of the Association of Chief Police Officers and the Commission for Racial Equality.

The Government's response to recommendations of the Parliamentary Select Committee was:–

"The Committee expressed concern at a deterioration of relations between sections of the West Indian community and the police and took the view that while there was a need for further relevant research, the latter would not in itself be adequate. In this context the Committee recommended that "the Home Secretary should invite the Commission for Racial Equality to set up a working party, on which representatives of both the police and the West Indian community should be members, to examine the continuing un-satisfactory relations between the police and the West Indian communities and to make recomendations for practical steps to secure their enforcement. The working party should consult the Home Office Advisory Committee on Race Relations Research about research which they consider would assist them in their enquiry.

"The Government shares the Committee's concern about the situation described in their report, especially as it affects young West Indians. It is in everyone's interest to try to improve relations; and the police, the West Indian community itself and all those involved must play their part in this . . . The Government therefore welcomes and has encouraged the links which in many parts of the country have been established at local levels between the police, community relations councils and the local community, including West Indian and other ethnic minority groups . . . . Regular liaison can help identify and deal with issues and uncertainties as they arise, and many police forces have appointed police community liaison officers to co-ordinate and stimulate such liaison.

"The Government's view is that since these problems are best discussed and where possible resolved through meetings at local and national level, the creation of a formal working party at this time to inquire generally would not be the best means of encouraging among

all those involved the degree of co-operation, understanding and good relations which the Government, like the Select Committee, is anxious to see."[50]

The implications that the members of a Black community were not yet ready for mature and constructive dialogue with the police and that profitable discussion could only take place with the white-dominated race relations bureaucracy may not have been the one the Government wished to convey; but the fact that neither the Government nor the CRE perceived that implication was alarming to say the least. It signalled to Black youth that their elders, and the leaders in the Black community had no status where the white bureaucracy was concerned. It suggested that when it came to serious and meaningful conversation, whites were only prepared to talk to other whites.

The Special Patrol Group the Police emergency unit, much in evidence in crowd control situations but also used on other occasions, has come in for considerable criticism. Its use in Southall during the 1979 election campaign brought it into conflict with the otherwise peaceful Asian community as the Commission for Racial Equality pointed out.[51] It was in this situation that Blair Peach, a white New Zealand born anti-racist campaigner, lost his life. John Brown, in a general assessment of the usefulness of the Special Patrol Group (SPG) said:–

"For most home beat officers, the losses of the SPG in action, in terms of community relations already out-weighs its benefits in terms of crime prevention. What's the good of short-term solutions that leave long-term problems of fouled-up working relationships."[52]

In a recently published booklet, *Youth in a Multi-Racial Society*, the Commission for Racial Equality has said that the use of "SUS" powers by the police had emerged as the single most important matter of concern in the relationships between the police and the minority communities.

The Commission although concerned by the number of Blacks arrested under this charge does not believe that the real answer to the problem was simply to repeal the 1824 Vagrancy Act. If, as much of the evidence suggests, the Act had been used in a discriminatory way, to harass young Blacks, then its mere removal would not end the discriminatory practice as police officers would simply find another way of fulfilling that prejudice. A clue to what is actually happening may rest in careful analysis of the differential use of the charge by different divisions even of the same force.[53]

But nowhere is the general disaffection more starkly shown than in the low numbers of ethnic minority people who join the police force and make a career out of policing. At the end of 1978 the strength of the Metropolitan Police Force was 22,197 of whom only 94 were from ethnic minority groups. The total police establishment in England and Wales was 90,352, of these 218 were from ethnic minority groups. The following table shows how this strength has developed and reflects the effects of special advertising campaigns in late 1975 and early 1976.[54]

Table 10
Police Forces in England and Wales
Police Officers from the ethnic minorities

Date	Metropolitan Police Only	All Forces
31.12.74	37	109
31.12.75	39	134
31.12.76	71	182
31.12.77	82	199
31.12.78	94	218

Source: Home Office Statistics

But it is not only by the police that the Black community is badly served. The law and order issues also enter the court room. Blacks are more likely to receive custodial sentences than their white counterparts. Custodial sentences where given to both Blacks and whites for similar offences are likely to be longer in the case of Blacks. Many young Blacks complain of inadequate legal representation and feel that the system of "plea bargaining" is abused.

Peter Warren is his study of the Wolverhampton scene concluded that from his unique position as a probation officer, no other person, not even a defending solicitor, and much less a barrister, had such a ringside seat and a closer contact with the defendant, especially when the defendant was a known client. He says:–

"Many Black youths complain that the legal aid solicitors and barristers do not defend them adequately. The observed perform-ances of solicitors in courts is frequently so poor that this criticism is in many cases felt to be justified. Some solicitors do little more than suggest that the magistrates follow the recommendations made by the Probation Officer in the social enquiry report. In the Crown

Court barristers do little better. The author has witnessed some blatant "plea bargaining" which almost amounts to conspiracy to pervert the course of justice.

"In both Magistrates Courts and Crown Courts the evidence which defendng solicitors and barristers appear most unwilling to challenge is evidence of assault on police officers. So neurotic are the Courts regarding their duty to protect the police from assault that they cannot perceive at all that they also have a duty to protect the defendant from assault by police. The incredibility with which the Courts look on evidence of police brutality is such that it is virtually impossible for any defendant to succeed in proving that he has been brutalised by police, although very rarely he may be acquitted on the grounds that the case against him has not been proved beyond all doubt."[55]

THE BLACK RESPONSE

An analysis of the way in which the British Empire was held together by the process of "divide and rule" among the natives will explain the obsession white society has in detailing the minutest differences between Black groups. White society' smugness in not giving Blacks their rights is cemented in the belief that so heterogeneous a collection of communities could not possibly coalesce to make an effective demand on the system. Throughout the literature a level of unanimity among Blacks is sought as a criterion for success which is nowhere to be found in white society.

The fact is not so much the differences that exist among Blacks, but that they were totally unprepared for what they found and that they have never been allowed to work out their own response. Blacks came to Britain with a presumption of British fair play and Christian tolerance. They came to assist the "Mother Country" in her post-war reconstruction and in return to provide for their children a brighter future.

For the treatment of the early immigrant response one turns to Part V of Rose et al, in *Colour and Citizenship.*[56] They set out the difference between the Indian Workers Association, based as it was on a largely Punjabi immigrant population, and the influence of the Indian High Commissioner upon it; and the Standing Conference of West Indian Organisations and its links with the Migrant Services Division of the West Indian Federal High Commission. Of these early beginnings they observed that in so far as the Indian immigrants were concerned the migration was homogeneous in its origin and led to a high degree of conformity with values held in common. Thus the internal organisation of the community with its strong emphasis on kinship ties and network of mutual obligation, helped to draw individuals into participation with the Indian Workers Association (IWA). On the other hand, the West Indian Standing Conference was a creation of the Migrant Service Division of the West Indian High Commission. It was attended by both West Indians and their white sympathisers. Among its affiliates were sports clubs, social welfare bodies, and inter-racial organisations set up on the initiative of white organisations like the parliamentary lobby known as the British Caribbean Association. The initial trend was certainly towards achieving integration, but the collapse of the West Indian Federation and the passing of the Commonwealth Immigration Act 1962 undermined the presumptions of British fair play which had dominated the scene.

The euphoria of the Labour victory in 1964 did not last long and Rose et al, Rex and Moore and sundry others wrote of the powerlessness and lack of leadership of the immigrant population. Indeed Neville Maxwell in a statement produced for the West Indian Standing Conference in 1965 said:–

"By and large, the West Indian until recently has been concerned less with the self-identification, West Indianism, negritude, or call-it-what-you-will, than with the unconscious drive to establish a minimal level of communication with the mature community. But now he has no alternative; white leadership and white perceptions of the Negro's part in British society are equally damaging to his future prospects in Britain." [57]

Mullard, in his assessment of *Colour and Citizenship,* says that the chief criticism can be summed up in one word – orientation. He contends that the whole section on the "immigrant response" is nothing more than a statement of how white sociologists see it. He adds:–

"The white liberal argues that while the Black occupies a minority position in society the white majority, racist or not, has the undeniable right to dictate policy, to have majority representation on official race groups. I disagree." [58]

"The West Indian with his Christian tradition and use of English as his basic language was completely unprepared for what Neville Maxwell described as "white leadership and white perceptions of the Negro's place in British Society." It has taken some time for the West Indian community to come to terms with this rejection and to stop trying to "gate-crash", as it were, into British society.

The Asian on the other hand was equally stunned by the failure of British society to accept his culture as different but of equal worth. Although in the beginning their internal organisation and strong emphasis on kinship ties prevented as traumatic an experience as that faced by the West Indians, in the end white society's message was clear. They were not only different, they were inferior.

While white liberals were obviously anxious over the treatment Blacks were receiving from their kith and kin, they evidently subscribed to the conviction that in a white majority society it was the unquestioned right of the whites to dictate the policy of change. Not only did they take this view with regard to the race relations bureaucracy but even when Blacks sought to initiate the Campaign Against Racial Discrimination (CARD) they jumped on the bandwagon and seized control.

Martin Luther-King visited Britain in 1964 on his way to Oslo to collect the Nobel Peace Prize. His meeting with David Pitt and other immigrant leaders gave birth to the Campaign Against Racial Discrimination. The history of CARD is best documented by Ben Heinemann,[59] and Rose et al already referred to. Heinemann contends that its collapse arose out of a conflict over control – Black or white. The white liberals, people who had been quick to jump on the bandwagon of a mass voluntary movement of Blacks that through its inspiration from Martin Luther-King seemed committed to non-violence, were able to mobilize support which would never have followed Black leadership. They raised funds from white sources, had contacts with press and television, and whilst their dedication, ability and political know-how were respected by the Black members, it was clear that the white liberals had taken over the organisation and CARD had become yet another Black dream.

What killed this last voluntary experiment of a non-Governmental multi-racial approach to racism in British society was the reaction of the white liberals when in 1967 Black members gained a substantial majority on the executive. The white liberals walked out of CARD with great trumpeting using the same press and television they had so shortly before used in the interest of the organisation. The support they had been able to mobilize proved as fickle and demonstrated that their commitment was to the white liberals in CARD and not what CARD stood for or represented.

As far as white liberals were concerned the simple act of democratically voting Blacks into the leadership of CARD was an

121

act of extremism. The official bodies with the support of local white liberals so dominated the local scene that CARD found it difficult to organise local Black cells. As Mullard contended, they possessed the power to dub CARD groups as extremist, to control the mass media, to prevent local authorities from helping CARD and even launched police campaigns against Blacks.[60] CARD was dead. It was murdered in cold blood by the brutal efficiency of the white liberals its Black members had learned to admire. Every Black attempt to regroup has floundered on this gigantic iceberg of official race relations institutions.

Time and again Blacks attempted new alliances and time and again they ran into the same difficulty. If whites were there, they were there because they were in the leadership role. If they could not have that role then they undermined the organisation and the movement. Michael Dummett one of the few whites who remained with CARD to the bitter end who has followed the demise of subsequent Black attempts to create a coherent articulate voice has pointed to three strategies used by the establishment to frustrate Blacks in their efforts. He lists them as (1) exploitation of cultural and linguistic differences; (2) luring the potential leaders into the official race bureaucracy; and (3) starving the organisations of funds.[61] Indeed Blacks have begun to measure the usefulness of a project to the Black community by the ease and speed with which the establishment is willing to fund. It is relatively easy to acquire funding for welfare activity which the authority ought to have provided in any case, but very difficult to get support for genuine community development.

While therefore some support has been given to a number of individual self-help projects up and down the country, funding for a coordinating and supportive structure that would provide a collective mechanism for helping these groups to respond coherently to the vital issues facing the community was being withheld.

It is clear that white society which has not yet come to grips with its own inequalities can hardly be expected to correct the inequalities it imposes on Blacks as an act of Christian charity. If Blacks feel equality is worth having, then they will not get it because white soiety has given it to them but because they have earned it.

One result of the crisis of confidence between the Black community and the Labour Party which followed the events of 1964 was the virtual opting out of the traditional political system. Ten years later in 1974 the CRE survey revealed that some 37 per cent of Afro-Caribbean and 27 per cent of Asians compared with 6 per cent of the white population were not on the electoral list. Despite that it revealed that the ethnic minorities played a significant part in determining the outcome of the election; that they swing more to Labour than the electorate as a whole, and that although most members of the minorities conformed with their socio-economic group in voting Labour, where other parties made an effort to gain their support this usually brought good results. In post-war years both the Labour and Liberal Parties have put forward ethnic minority candidates although the Conservatives until then had not done so.[62]

One apparent result of that report was the setting up by the Conservatives of the Anglo-Indian Conservative Society and the Anglo-West Indian Conservative Society in an effort to mobilize Conservative opinion among the ethnic minority. This was done around ethnic minority councillors who were already taking the Tory whip. Although still under-represented since 1974, ethnic minority candidates had started to appear more frequently in local elections and the numbers of local councillors from the ethnic minority groups has grown steadily.

An Opinion Research Centre survey conducted in 1974 revealed that where the candidate was a West Indian or an Asian, one out of four traditional Labour voters were no longer prepared to vote along party lines. This compared with three out of eight Conservatives.[63]

This confirms the case of Dr David Pitt who stood as the Labour candidate in the "safe" Labour seat of Clapham in 1970 and suffered a defeat with a 10.2 per cent swing from Labour to the Conservatives, twice the swing in the surrounding constituencies.[64]

A more recent survey has been done by Muhammed Anwar of the Commission for Racial Equality. The survey covered 24 inner-city constituencies; nine in London, six in the Midlands, six in the North, two in the South and one in Scotland. He concluded that the concentration of the ethnic vote helped Labour hang on to seats that would have otherwise gove to the Conservatives. If the national result had been closer, the ethnic vote could have once again won it for Labour. Ethnic minority registration had gone up on 1974 with the Afro-Caribbean registration moving from the 63 per cent to 81 per cent and the Asian from 73 per cent to 77 per cent. However, once registered the Asian was more likely to

Table 11
Ethnic Minority Candidates in Recent General Elections

	Labour	Liberal	Conservative	Fringe
1970*	Dr. Pitt	Pritam Singh	–	Dharam Dass
	–	Mihir Gupta	–	Saeed-Uu-Zafar
	–	Ghulam Musa	–	Tonderai Makoni
Feb. 1974	Bashi Mann	Dhani Prem	–	Balder Singh Chatel
	–	–	–	Tariq Ali
Oct. 1974	–	Cecil Williams	–	Sylvester Smart
	–	–	–	Elias Browne
	–	–	–	Chandra Rao
1979	Russell Profitt	Cecil Williams	Farooq Saleem	James Hunte
		Raj Mal Singh	Maj. N. Saroop	

Source: CRE. Votes and Policies 1980

vote than the West Indian.[65]

One consequence of the growing number of Black councillors is the development of a Black Caucus of councillors across party lines. On April 21, 1979, they convened the first ever Black People's Manifesto Conference. The conference approved the first Black People's Manifesto. It outlined the problems of Black people in Britain and demanded action on sixteen specific issues which would promote racial equality. The manifesto was sent both to the leaders of the major political parties as well as to candidates who were standing in areas with concentrations of Black electors.[66] Anwar also discussed the role of the Standing Conference of Pakistani Organisations (SCOPO) which advised its members and other Pakistanis to vote Liberal in constituencies where the Liberal candidate had a chance of winning, but otherwise to vote Labour. In contrast, the President of the Confederation of Indian Organisations made a public plea for Asians to vote Conservative: In addition he described a very active ethnic minority press and concluded:

"... ethnic minority communities participated fully in the General Election campaign as well as in the actual elections either through the ethnic minority organisations to which they belong, through the ethnic minority press in which matters pertaining to race relations *and immigration featured significantly or took part in the campaigning activities of the main political parties. It is clear from our data that their influence in the political life of the nation is likely to increase in the future rather than decrease, especially as the majority of voters and candidates we surveyed welcome their participation.* [67]

In his introductory statement for the Council of Churches, Gus John points out that Britain's treatment of Blacks illustrates three important things. Firstly, that Britain saw Black immigrants as little more than second-class production factors: as labour stock whose yield could be maximised, given the social circumstances they encounter . . . . higher rents, higher HP, in fact the privilege of being Black entitled you to work longer hours and pay more for everything.

Secondly, because of the society's attitude to and way of seeing Black people, it was felt that it was quite acceptable to consign them to urban areas already disintegrating with decay, and rumbling more with the conflict generated by dispossessed groups aspiring towards a more humane way of life. Black people were lumped, lock stock and barrell with the white working class. The society then turned round and blamed the Blacks for the urban decay and for the results of social inaction and unplanned urban growth on the part of successive Governments.

Thirdly, that Britain, through refusing to come to terms with its own history and to accept that it was essentially a racist society, had laid its increasing social problems – most of which were a function of the racialist nature of the society – at the door of "the alien wedge".

He concluded by saying:–

"We cannot, therefore, allow white society to dictate the terms of analysis of our situation in Britain, nor give the prescriptions. So long as we continue to latch on to the remedies white society prescribes for us we shall continue to enhance our own destruction, for I can think of few occasions in which Britain has done something in response to the Black situation which was not dictated by self-interest and geared ultimately to saving itself." [68]

Speaking of the response of Asian women in particular, Amrit Wilson writes:–

"They may feel that when oppressed they are being oppressed as individuals, but racism is an attack on them as a part of their family and community, and these things cannot be separated in the

125

identity of a woman."
and adds:–

>*"There is hope because women are beginning to perceive that there can be a happier future and because they have such spirit and because their anger is growing. How long it will take for a strong movement to merge is impossible to say, these are early, early days in a conscious struggle."*[69]

Blacks in Britain are aware of the struggle that must now be fought in the interest of their children's future, but they have no illusions of either the magnitude of the task or the nature of the enemy. The West Indian poet, Claude McKay, expressed it in these lines:–

>*"If we must die, let it not be like hogs*
>*Hunted and penned in an inglorious spot . . . .*
>*If we must die, O let us nobly die,*
>*. . . . though far outnumbered let us show brave*
>*And for their thousand blows deal one death blow*
>*. . . like men we will face the murderous cowardly pack*
>*Pursued to the wall, dying, but fighting back,*
>*We will never attack first."*[70]

"It is time for all of us to tell each other the truth about who and what have brought the Negro to the condition of deprivation against which he struggles today. In human relations the truth is hard to come by, because most groups are deceived about themselves. Rationalisation and incessant search for scapegoats are the psychological cataracts that blind us to our individual and collective sins. But the day has passed for bland euphemisms. He who lives with untruth lives in spiritual slavery. Freedom is still the bonus we receive for knowing the truth.

King, Martin Luther.
Chaos of Community?
London. Hodder & Stoughton, 1967, p.67

CHAPTER 7

THE YEARS AHEAD

INTER-RELATION BETWEEN THE FIVE AREAS of STUDY
Before discussing the years ahead, the author wishes to draw attention to the inter-relation between the five areas of his concern – the economic, educational, housing, social welfare and political. Blacks had set out to Britain with high hopes if not for themselves then certainly for the new life they would be able to offer their children. Their economic vistas were high but as Smith and others have shown they faced a level of discrimination that prevented them from attaining the stake in the job market which their talents and skills would have justified and which had there been some scope for upward mobility they would have reached with the passage of time.

Cross cites that they were referred to by many as the new proletariat and were thus confirmed on the lower rung of the socio-economic ladder. This of course had a profound effect on their earning capacity and level of the services and amenities they could buy. The fact that there was no coherent migrant strategy meant that they settled near to the factories in which they worked and because of the extent of racial prejudice operating in the housing market they got trapped in the least desirable housing. So while lack of political foresight and employment demand pulled them into inner city housing, the forces of racial discrimination blocked their advance at work and limited their movement within the housing market.

But where they lived determined the schools their children attended. The study has shown that inner city schools were more likely to be older, less attractive, less well supplied with up-to-date libraries and other facilities and to have a high turnover of teachers. In short, the educational opportunity was not as great as in surburban schools. If one added to that the attitude of teachers and in many cases their low expectations of Blacks, it is easy to see how in the absence of clear political direction Black children became disadvantaged at school. In turn the lack of educational performance would affect the employability and status in society with its consequent effect on the homes they would be able to acquire for themselves and their own families. And thus, unless checked, the cycle of deprivation would continue.

Indeed the stress from these circumstances reflected in the demands being made on the social services. As the pressures of cultural conflict increased, unclear political objectives and the break-down of the extended family system gave rise to new social needs to which the social services were unaccustomed and to which they were slow to respond.

The study reveals that a lack of political acceptance of the level of racism in the society directed all the force of Government in the direction of policies which were widely interpreted as Government's endorsement of a second class citizenship for Blacks. However much each Government sought to deny it and however lofty their words, their actions showed an acceptance of the principle that too many Blacks were a danger to the country. The rest that followed flowed naturally from that viewpoint.

Redressing the imbalances faced by Black Britain will not be easy, nor is it likely to be immediate. What needs to be done in the years ahead will take both time and commitment, but if there is no starting there can be no ending. The street disturbances in the Summer of 1981 have added an urgency to the search for solutions. They constituted the latest warning of the consequences of benign neglect. This chapter is devoted to the task before us. There is much that both white institutions and Black organisations can do to significantly improve the quality of life for Black Britain and to ensure that St Paul's of 1980 and Brixton, Southall and Liverpool of 1981 do not become a normal feature of British society.

ECONOMIC ISSUES

If Black Britain is ever to achieve its rightful position in British society it will be necessary for it to attain a greater stake through-out the economic field. To do this a way must be found to lessen the effects of racial discrimination in employment and employers must recognise that the instituting of equal opportunity programmes are as much in their own interests as they are useful for the fuller integration of Blacks into the society.

Equal opportunity policies must be more than pious statements of interest. Both trade unions and managements must see them as an integral part of their negotiation framework and regulations for annual reviews and ongoing monitoring of the programmes must be explicitly included in the arrangements. Experience during the early years of the 1976 Race Relations Act has revealed that a number of companies with equal opportunity policies have continued to be found guilty of individual acts of racial discrimination largely because no effective monitoring system existed.

These policies and the programmes that flow from them, must relate not only to recruitment but also to promotion and training, and all other areas related to the job situation. They must be fully communicated throughout the workforce. Both Central and local government as major employers will need to take a lead in this and their failure so far to do so will need to be the centrepiece of any campaign which develops in the future. Both the Civil Service and the corps of local government officers need to be more representative of the multiracial nature of modern British society.

Black workers have to devise a strategy for using their collective power within the framework of the trade union movement and thus stopping the movement from functioning as it currently does as a white man's movement rather than an organisation of all workers regardless of race, colour or sex. Only with the full willing support of the trade unions can the society eliminate racial discrimination in employment and take the necessary steps towards equality of opportunity in jobs. But this support will not just be given, it has to be earned.

While all must reject the concept of Black unions, there is a strong argument for Blacks to have a strategy of operation in order to affect the fullest possible participation in trade union affairs and this should begin with ensuring that all trade unions as a matter of urgency should review their recruitment policies and their service delivery as it relates to their Black membership.

The TUC Charter for Black Workers, published in 1981, will fail unless Black workers themselves mobilise within the trade union movement to ensure that the Charter becomes an effective tool for progress. Not only must they organise to take an active part in their trade union branches and seek office within them, they must also ensure that in the total education programme for shop stewards and branch officials, all unions integrate race and community relations issues.

The failure to date of Black Britain to produce a collective response to its plight in employment has been partly attributed to the fact that the process of racial discrimination to which they have been subjected have been so subtle as to leave the victims believing that their plight was a result of their own inadequacies. It has also been argued that because Blacks occupy those jobs which whites no longer wanted, that their contribution to the survival of the national economy is negligible.

The truth is that Blacks occupy key jobs – even if not well paid – in vital sectors of the economy. It would be useful – if not educative – to remind the nation and the Black community itself of this fact. A "Black Workers' Day" observed annually would call attention to the role of the Black worker in maintaining the growth of the economy, and hence the justification for his demands for a fair slice of the national cake. It would provide a focus for Black workers to review their relationship with the trade union movement and a platform from which they could address themselves collectively to the trade union movement as a whole. It could articulate the major trade union challenges as Blacks saw them for the ensuing year.

It is doubtful whether the trade union movement will welcome this initiative in the first instance, but be that as it may, Black workers must judge it on its merit and worth to them. They must determine to exert their influence positively and to stamp their imprint on the development on working class freedom.

The Commission for Racial Equality must use its power of investigation far more rigorously against those employers and their allies who persist in discriminatory practices. Their targets should be chosen from amongst those whose place in society would lead to a ripple effect causing the consequences of the investigations to be felt well beyond the plant or company investigated. Linked to this more aggressive strategy should be a sustained campaign to encourage black workers who are discriminated against to take action before industrial tribunals under the 1976 Race Relations Act. This would not only act to enhance the law, but also substantially heighten the awareness of those responsible for man-management in the employment field.

The development of business enterprises is an essential strategy to the enhancement of community self-esteem. Anwar, in his study of Pakistanis in Britain, *The Myth of Return*, argues that it is not only "the sense of prosperity, independence and respect which being self-employed brought them in this community", but also what being an employer could mean in the reversal of roles that was important in the relationship between Blacks and whites in the community. It is now generally accepted that so long as Blacks remain "the employed" and never "the employer" so long can they expect to be discriminated against with impunity.

But as the evidence has shown, the traditional sources of finance were not going to make it possible for them to embark on this course, and those who have, have had to do so at great odds. The growth and interlocking relationship of the larger internationals, the chain stores and supermarkets coupled to a repressive taxation, have virtually put paid to the "rags to riches" entrepreneurial adventurist. And this despite all the Thatcher Government's supposed commitment to small businesses.

The Parliamentary Home Affairs Committee, which visited the USA in 1980, returned enthused with what the US Federal Government was doing to stimulate the growth of small businesses within the Black community there.[1] The author has long held the view that the creation of a Black managerial class tied to the development of business enterprises was crucial to the elimination of racial discrimination and the development of equality of opportunity.

The Black community must seek much more than the Home Affairs Committee in its report on Racial Disadvantage, published in 1981, is prepared to offer. If the Government is committed to seeing the development of a vibrant Black sector in the business community then it must not only ensure the availability of the necessary capital to stimulate the creation of these enterprises and to promote the training of their managers, it must also be prepared – and the Black community must insist on this – to regulate its contracts to ensure that a fair share of its works reaches these businesses either direct or by sub-contract.

A useful structure would be the creation of a Black Small Business Finance Bureau capable of funding low-cost loans for the setting up of small businesses employing up to 250 people with preference being shown to co-operative societies. The Bureau should have an additional function of assisting with the training of managers and the development of managerial skills from among the sponsors. The Bureau's finance could be derived 50 per cent from the exchequer and 50 per cent from the traditional banking sources. The modest target over the first five years being in the area of 500 new businesses or 25,000 new jobs.

EDUCATION

A lot of the debate in the field of education has been centred on the concentration of Black pupils in a minority of schools. It has persisted despite the fact that it has been shown to be of little or no educational relevance. Politicians and others have been worried about the possible effects large numbers of Black kids still clinging to their cultural roots could have on white kids and white cultural patterns. Fortunately, despite official inducements and pressure from racialists, dispersal has never gained ground. The sad fact, however, is that we are still a long way from convincing educational administrators that Black cultures may be different but they are not inferior. The prime aim in modern curriculum development remains the attainment of a truly integrated multi-cultural syllabus.

Teacher attitudes and their general low expectation of West Indian children in particular, together with the lack of appropriate training for teaching in a multi-cultural, multi-racial situation have done much to reinforce the handicap of a deficient socio-economic background and contribute to a disproportionate representation of Blacks in schools for the educationally sub-normal and other areas of underachievement.

In so far as teacher-training is concerned, all students on teacher training, whether on initial or post-graduate courses, should be made to recognise that wherever they might go to teach, they would do so in a multi-cultural society. This is simply a basic realisation of what Britain now is. Indeed it is a failure to come to terms with that reality that has kept so much of our education ethnocentric and has acted as a brake on the speedier development of genuine multi-cultural curricula.

As a further aid to quicker adjustments and the bridging of Home-School relationships, the development of special Home-School teams will be found to be helpful to teachers, parents and children. While there is some merit in the argument that this is only a temporary problem, there will certainly be need for them throughout the 1980s.

If Black groups are to avoid merely papering over the cracks caused by bad social planning and a system which discriminates against them, then they must unite in a way capable of producing genuine community development programmes. In the final analysis, if local education authorities do not respond positively in the immediate future, serious thought will have to be given to extending the range of educational schemes from head-start to supplementary classes to the actual operation of regular schools. They may be the only way of demonstrating that the reason for head-start programmes and supplementary classes has been the failure of the educational system to their children in the first place.

Black communities must themselves take part in determining how Black history and culture finds its way into any multi-cultural syllabus. This is an area in which the community is able to make a considerable contribution.

Society will ignore the needs of the growing number of alienated Black youth to its peril, and more than lip service needs to be given to the development of community self-help. Local education authorities must come to terms with the need for training more Black youth leaders and raising the level of Black participation in the youth service. They will not be able to achieve that goal without paying cognisance to the cultural norms of control which various groups within the Black community exercise over their children. The level of Black alienation is alarming, and if the youth club provision is ever to meet this situation, it must be more than a resource for communal leisure facility, but also a societal means of support and counselling.

The Race Relations lobby, Chief Education Officers and the Parliamentary Select Committee on Race Relations and Immigration have all cried out for more resources, and in some cases for a special fund, to meet the special educational needs of immigrant children. Except the money allocated as an inducement for dispersal and some for staffing, successive Governments have been reluctant to create special funding for fear of white resenment and have relied on funding Inner City disadvantage in the belief that since the majority of Blacks live in these areas they would be bound to benefit from any general assault on disadvantage.

But certainly such a belief misses the central issue. The addtional resources were being put at the disposal of the same policy makers and resource distributors who had ignored and neglected Black needs. It is the author's contention that what is needed in the first instance is not additional financial resources but a fundamental re-think of educational objectives and curriculum demands for a multi-cultural society.

Such a review would bring about a re-allocation of existing resources. What the author is recommending and calling for is not more courses, but a sensitive adjustment in the content of existing courses; a re-orientation of the spending on school libraries, and on the history, literature, art, drama and music used in schools.

The progress that has been made, has been made by those teachers who have accepted the challenge of teaching both in and for a multi-cultural society. They are the indispensible human resources that need to be captured. It is their commitment and attitudes, which, if correctly harnessed and supported by administrators equally committed to redressing the balance of past inequality, will meet the needs of all.

HOUSING

Black Britain has found itself concentrated in the lower end of the housing market with the vast majority of its members living in inner city areas closely identified with physical and social disintegration. Most local authorities, because of a lack of adequate information for policy determination, have not been able to plan for the special needs of Blacks in such areas as homelessness among West Indian youth, homeless teenage Asian girls, one-parent families, ethnic elderly and multi-generation families.

Because factors other than housing needs have up to now affected access to public housing, Black Britain has found that despite its housing need, it has obtained less than its fair share of public housing and that even where it has been able to gain access, the quality of housing it acquired was on average the less desirable. In the private sector a combination of free market economic forces in which Black Britain was less able to compete on an equal footing and a variety of subtle devices of racial discrimination resulted in a loss of freedom of upward mobility in the housing market.

Having thus locked Black Britain in certain areas, white society grew wary of the potential political strength this provided and sought to reverse the process through dispersal without necessarily improving the housing position of Blacks. To overcome this state of affairs, local authorities as a major actor in this sphere, must collect information on ethnic minorities which would enable them to identify the housing position of various groups, together with any special needs in existence, and any difficulties arising either from those needs or the attempts which might be made to meet them.

But this may not be all. Communication with Blacks on the complexities of the housing market has been weak and there has been a reluctance on the part of local authorities to keep ethnic records and more importantly to monitor the effects of their service delivery to Black Britain. It is essential therefore that those local authorities with significant numbers of Black residents should review their communication policies to ensure that their housing provision is adequately presented to those residents who may be in housing need. In some cases this may lead to the appointment of staff with competence in languages other than English or the production of promotional material in the mother-tongue of their residents.

Housing Associations and other community projects because of their greater management flexibility, and their need to respond to local situations are well suited to assist with some of the special needs which crop up in the Black community. In assisting and supporting these schemes, the local authority has a responsibility to ensure that the quality of service is no less than if the local authority were itself providing the service. Black groups may increasingly find it advantageous to make alliances with housing associations already specialising in areas of special needs. In this way they may be able to exploit the housing association structure in meeting some of the needs of their communities.

There are two initiatives which Central Government must take if Black Britain is ever to assume that there is a commitment to come to terms with housing conditions in the Black community. Firstly, the Department of the Environment, the Ministry with responsibility for both planning and housing, should set up a Working Party on Race Relations consisting of representatives of the Black ethnic minority groups, race relations agencies and officials from various relevant divisions of the Department. The Working Party should not only have an advisory function but should also review the full range of Black housing needs and the strategies employed to meet them.

Secondly, in its support of local authority housing schemes, Central Government should insist on a number of things from the local authority. It should be satisfied that the authority has in arriving at its decisions used an adequate data-base to allow it to determine the needs of its Black population. It should also be able to demonstrate that it sees Black housing need as part of its wider arrangement for housing management and related problems.

SOCIAL SERVICES

We have seen how the failure to accept the role of racial discrimination in service delivery has rendered the social services departments impotent in many areas. The cultural distinctiveness of the Black communities has survived and that added to the presence of prejudice and discrimination has given rise to a number of special needs within the Black community.

To meet this situation social services agencies should re-evaluate their policies, strategies and practices at two levels to ensure that they are keeping pace with our modern multi-cultural society. Firstly at the level of perspectives and skills to enhance their service delivery in general and in particular to ensure meeting the needs of the Black community. Secondly, they should do so at the level of management structures to promote the development of appropriate machinery to good race relations practice.

The inability of the agencies to deal adequately with the special needs of Black groups has added impetus to self-help strategies from within the communities themselves which have so far received only lukewarm support from the authorities. Two courses of action recommend themselves. First, as a part of their efforts to make their services more responsive to Black community needs, social work agencies in consultation with the Black community should identify the key special issues for social workers in their areas. Some of this is already being done by a few agencies, but the response is as yet too patchy. More important still is the need for local authorities to rethink their approach to Black self-help and align their support in keeping with the objective of improving the quality of community involvement and participation. Too much of what is currently done is individual project oriented, piecemeal and not related to any coherent strategy.

Although recognised by the policy-makers, the need for adequate staffing and appropriate training to meet the challenge of a multi-cultural clientele has not been met. Considering the personal nature of much of what the service is about, this failure is in itself a form of racial discrimination. Social services agencies must therefore seek to recruit Black staff and so end the current under-representation of Black people in the staffing of the various agencies, as well as increase the number of Black trainees they recruit. The agency can hardly expect to be credible in its claim to be caring, understanding, sympathetic and sensitive until it has done this.

But this is not a plea for the lowering of standards, and any shortage of trained Black staff must be a challenge to those responsible for accepting students into social and community work training courses to bear in mind the need for increasing the number of Black social and community workers. Social work agencies and the training institutions involved need to work out arrangements whereby they can together take the appropriate measures for training potential ethnic minority staff as provided for within the 1976 Race Relations Act.[2]

In order to make training relevant to the needs of our multicultural society it is important that all social work training courses should contain the following four elements:–

a) *Basic knowledge of the culture of ethnic minorities in Britain.*

b) *An examination of the relevance of traditional social work skills to work with ethnic minorities along with the possibilities of extending the range and type of skills so that more appropriate responses might be available to ethnic minority clients.*

c) *Key issues raising special needs in ethnic minority groups.*

d) *The effects of prejudice and racial discrimination.*

The economic depression of the last few years has laid great stress on the lower paid and increased pressure on the social services. Cuts imposed on local authority spending have limited the resources available and in the absence of any coherent database for decision making the needs of many Black groups have not been met. This has certainly compounded the disadvantage already prevalent from racial discrimination.

POLITICAL ISSUES

It would be helpful to re-state here the author's hypothesis that the Government's overall strategy in race and community relations will not achieve its stated objectives of harmony and equality of opportunity for Blacks since racial discrimination – the major factor inhibiting progress – is still not recognised for the cancer it is. Lord Scarman in his report on the 1981 disturbances categorically denies the existence of "institutional racism".[3] It is clear from the review of the literature that while successive Governments have taken steps towards outlawing racial discrimination on the one hand, the same Governments have on the other hand passed other legislation that has been equally discriminatory in effect.

Although Britain was receiving a steady flow of immigrants from the Commonwealth to meet manpower needs, no coherent immigrant strategy was devised. It was only when forced to do so

137

through her desire to join the EEC that Britain began to look at immigration policy. The result was a racially discriminatory policy. None of the major political parties understood the extent of racial prejudice and an all-party consensus that good race relations in Britain depended upon limiting Black immigration emerged almost without anyone knowing it had.

The anti-immigrant vote of the extreme right represents but a small part of the total anti-immigrant vote. The major parties seek to hold their anti-immigrant voters by adopting various racialist stances. The size of the ultra-right groups is consequently a function of the extent to which the major parties have accommodated anti-immigrant views.

Successive British Governments since 1962 have pursued an immigration control strategy geared to drastically reducing the intake of Blacks. Each new regulation has further restricted the value of the British passport to the Black Commonwealth citizens and seriously called into question the 1948 Nationality Act. The Tory Government in 1979 was quick to bring in a new nationality law which transferred the racist elements of the existing immigration legislation into the new Nationality Act. It created three classes of citizens with different rights and privileges, and removed rights previously enjoyed by many of Britain's Blacks.

The politics of race had dictated that it was far more convenient to discuss immigration and immigrants than racial prejudice and discrimination. It made it possible for politicians to out-do each other in appealing to the basest human instincts for political expediency. Because of the political obsession with immigration it was possible for the racist lobby to push successive governments into more and more restrictive immigration policies. Now that this has given rise to a new nationality law only compulsory repatriation remains. The day when that too becomes politically respectable cannot be far off. Only the emergence of a single collective force in the form of a National Civil Rights movement led and controlled by Blacks and responsive to the ground-swell of Black needs can stave off that cruel day.

But such a movement will have a larger task than that. Because Government started off from the position that too many Blacks were a danger to racial harmony and pursued rigorous immigration control policy, the institutions which it created with the task of eliminating racial discrimination and promoting integration were destined to face tremendous difficulties and loss of a public credibility. The movement would therefore act as a spur to make their work that much more relevant and acceptable.

It could for example ensure that the Commission for Racial Equality took its responsibility for strategic investigations far more seriously. It could assist it with target determination far more relevant to the Black community, and thus stimulate its development of means for pursuing its investigations with more vigour. Indeed it would serve to enhance the role of Blacks and their influence within the Commission and provide the vehicle for the establishment of a joint consultative body between the Commission and the Black community. In addition, the Black-led Civil Rights movement would be capable of taking on the function of campaigning for those social, political and economic issues that affect the Black community. It would provide a collective articulate voice and form both an effective pressure group as well as an instrument of advocacy and representation.

It could facilitate the setting up of a Working Party between the police and the Black community. The Government should now be willing to give its blessing to this. The Working Party should in addition be looking at the areas of tension between the police and the Black community. It should also explore the creation of schemes likely to produce areas of co-operation between the police and the community.

The police have borne the brunt of the law and order debate and much of the antagonism and resentment of the young Blacks in particular. Despite the efforts being made by some police forces to reduce the tensions between them and the Black community the police cannot escape a fair portion of the blame. One cannot help feeling, however, that Government could do more to create a sense of fairness and acceptance to full citizenship and thus create a sense of belonging and security which coupled with a sounder economic policy, would permit a more positive approach to the problems of Black youth.

Equally important is the need for the Black community to end its ambivalence to young Blacks joining the police force. Whatever the ills of the police force they will not be solved by Blacks staying out, and indeed the entry of Blacks into the service might prove a valuable impetus to their correction. It is only as the police force resembles more closely the normality of our multi-racial society throughout its ranks that we will have a sound basis for effecting fundamental change in relation to the way in which Blacks are treated. it would be a great step forward if the Black community would give support to a sustained campaign for the recruitment of Blacks into the police force. It is wholly illogical for Blacks to argue for equality of opportunity in all other spheres of public life and then maintain the police force as a prohibited area.

But it has to be borne in mind that there are other areas of the law and order system. Magistrates, solicitors, barristers, jurors, justices as well as the probation and prison services all play their part in the plight of Black Britain. It is important that they all carefully review the contribution and the attitude and mood that surrounds the part they play. In 1980 the West Midland Probation and After-Care Service published its own review.[4] Other services and groups need to do the same.

The paucity of Black magistrates emphasises the onesidedness of the scales of justice. Suitably qualified Blacks should be drafted to the Magistrate's bench and training for both lay and stipendary Magistrates should include modules on race relations. It is important that the dispensers of justice should understand how racial prejudice works and how it can cloud an otherwise sound judgement. Racial discrimination in the legal profession must be investigated and eliminated, and the utterances of the judiciary must be carefully monitored in order to deal effectively with the lapses of tainted statements of racial innuendo which sometimes come from those lofty heights. It is not acceptable for highly placed judges to suggest that Black jurors would be less than objective in dealing with cases in which Black defendants are involved. Such statements challenge not only the integrity of Blacks but also the validity of the jury system itself.

The funding strategy for Black needs has relied almost solely on local authority support. The local authorities have generally been reluctant to commit adequate funds for a variety of reasons and has used the schemes more frequently to further their own projects than meet the special needs within the Black communities. In the circumstances there is urgency in the call for the provision of a Central Government (Ethnic Needs) Fund providing 75 per cent Exchequer funds for special needs within the Black community. Funds could go either to local authorities or direct to voluntary group sponsors within the community. Where local authorities seek funds under this scheme they should demonstrate that they have consulted with the Black community in their area.

But meeting ethnic needs is not the sole responsibility of Government. Redressing the imbalances in society is a national problem. We must therefore witness before long the creation of a National Community Trust to stimulate and co-ordinate support from industry and commerce for schemes geared to promote equality of opportunity and Black community development. Such a Trust should seek and gain the full and active participation of the Black-led National Civil Rights movement.

There is evidence that far too few Blacks are being nominated for political office. There is evidence too, to show that the electorate in many areas is not yet ready for Black candidates. Political parties have an educational job to do in promoting themselves as truly democratic organisations. Recent elections have demonstrated the importance of the Black vote in many constituencies. They have also demonstrated that the Black vote has not as yet been used to the maximum. It would be one of the functions of a National Civil Rights movement to promote Black participation in the major political parties. Party affiliation must remain a personal choice, but once that choice is taken then opportunity for full involvement must be there.

Significantly, a Black caucus of local councillors is developing across party lines. In 1979, they convened the first ever Black Peoples' Manifesto Conference. They outlined the problems facing Black Britain and sought action on sixteen specific issues which in their view could promote racial equality. It was a hurried response to a suddenly called General Election, but it served notice on the major parties that the Black political machines was coming of age. That caucus must be developed in the years ahead.

The challenge that must now be met is that goals must be set as a matter of urgency for achieving Black members of Parliament. The Black community cannot and must not remain unrepresented. It must not tolerate a situation which approaches taxation without adequate representation. Nor can it rely upon the creation of life peerages as its sole means of representation in Parliament.

Equally, if not more importantly, is the rate with which the number of Black councillors has increased. The general objective would be to bring the number of Black councillors into broad balance with the proportion of Blacks within the various local authorities. To achieve this will require a greater level of political commitment and will from the major political parties than we have so far seen. It will also call for a new level of awareness from the Black community itself.

But wherever one turns one finds evidence of that new spirit of awareness among Blacks. They are aware of the struggle. They have begun to fight back for their freedom and dignity. Never has the spirit of self-sacrifice been greater. They are aware too of the nature of the enemy and that the struggle will be long. There is a new realism that some will die in the struggle before the journey's end; but what matters most is that the task of facing up to the challenge has begun.

REFERENCES

CHAPTER 1

1. Sheila Allen: *New Minorities, Old Conflicts: Asian and West Indian Migrants in Britain.* New York, Random House, 1971.
2. Allan N. Little: *Education Policies for Multi-racial Areas* London: Goldsmith College, London University 1978, p.5.
3. ICMC: Migration Information Services No. 11, Chapter 4, Figures 7/8, p.64.
4. Ibid.
5. Minority Rights Group, Report No. 28: Western European Migrant Workers, p.21.
6. Sheila Patterson: *Dark Strangers: A Study of West Indians in London.* London: Penguin Books 1965.
7. C. Jones: *Immigration and Social Policy in Britain*, London: Tavistock, 1977.
8. Home Office: *Racial Discrimination,* London HMSO 1975. Command 6234 . . B.
9. Quoted in The Inner City Education, Londn 3rd December 1976.
10. HMSO Select Committee on Race Relations & Immigration 1968-69 Report.
11. E.J.B. Rose: *Colour and Citizenship.* London OUP 1969, p.18.
12. Ibid, p.181.
13. CRC: *Unemployment and Homelessness. A Report.* London HMSO 1974.
14. David Smith: *Racial Disadvantage in Unemployment:* London: PEP 1974.
15. HMSO Second Report of the Commonwealth Immigration Advisory Council. Command 2266. London 1964.
16. HMSO *Hansard* 27th November 1963, Col. 434.
17. Cross, Crispin. *Ethnic Minorities in the Inner City.* London CRE 1977, p.123.
18. HMSO Hansard. House of Commons Report 6 April 1977, Col. 1236.
19. HMSO Policy for the Inner Cities.
20. Ibid.
21. HMSO Report on West Indian Community. London 1977.
22. Home Office. *Racial Discrimination.* London 1975. Command 6234.
23. Daniel, W.W. *Racial Discrimination in England.* London: Penguin Books. 1968.
24. Ibid.
25. CRE. *Five Views of Multiracial Britain.* London 1978, p.29.
26. Mullard, Chris. *Black Britain.* London. George Allen and Unwin 1973, p.41.
27. *Time.* Underclass in the Making. 20 August 1979.
28. Ibid, p.7.
29. Ibid, p.8.
30. Ibid. p.9.

143

CHAPTER 2

1. Cross, Crispin. Op cit, p.38.
2. Cross. Op cit, p.40.
3. PEP. *National Survey of Racial Minorities.* London 1974, p.110.
4. Smith, David. *Racial Disadvantage in Britain.* PEP. London 1977, p.72.
5. Cross, Crispin. Op cit. p.31.
6. Ibid p.75.
7. Smith, David. Op cit, p.81.
8. HMSO. *Department of Employment Gazette.* London 1963.
9. HMSO. *1971 Census, Advance Analysis.* London 1974.
10. Smith, David. Ibid, p.69.
11. Smith, Davd. Ibid, p.71.
12. Dept. of Employment Gazette, September 1975, p.868.
13. Brooks, Dennis. *Black Employment in the Black Country: A Study of Walsall.* London. Runneymede Trust 1975, p.8.
14. Smith, David. Op cit.
15. Ballard, Roger & Holden, Bronwen. *New Community* Vol. 10, No, 3 1975 pp.325-336 and "Racial Discrimination: No Room at the Top. *New Society* Vol. 32 No. 654 1975, pp. 133-135.
16. Taylor, J.H. "Newcastle-upon-Tyne Asian Pupils do Better than Whites". *British Journal of Sociology* Vol. 54, No. 4 1973.
17. Cross, C. op cit p. 44.
18. Jowell, Roger. Prescott-Clarke, Patricia. op cit.
19. Smith, David and McIntosh, Neil. *The Extent of Racial Discrimination.* London, PEP 1974, p.117.
20. *Time.* Underclass in the Making. 20 August 1979.
21. Wilson, Amrit. *Finding a Voice.* London, Virago 1978, p. 59.
22. Ibid, p. 70.
23. Ibid, p. 70.
24. Cross. Op cit, p. 47.
25. Dept. of Employment. *Table 7 Race Relations and Whites.* London HMSO 1972, p. 6-7.
26. Patterson Sheila. *Dark Strangers.* London, p. 152.
27. Anwar, Muhammed. *The Myth of Return.* London. Heinemann 1979 p. 125.
28. Ibid, p. 127.
29. Ibid, p. 128.
30. Allen, Sheila. Bornat, J. & Bently, S. *Work, Race and Immigration.* Bradford. University of Bradford 1977, p. 256.

CHAPTER 3

1. McNeal, Julia. "Education" in *The Prevention of Racial Discrimination in Britain.* S. Abbott (ed). London, Oxford University Press 1971, p. 111.
2. Cross, Crispin. op cit p. 79.
3. Townsend, H.E.R. & Britton, E.M. *Organisation in Multi-racial Schools.* London: NFER 19, p. 1.
4. HMSO. Circular 7/65, Department of Education and Science.
5. Mobey, C. *Social and Ethnic Mix n Schools and the Relationship With Attainment of Children aged 8 and 11.* London: Centre for Environmental Studies. Research Paper 9 1974.
6. Little, Alan. "The Educational Achievement of Ethnic Minority Children in London Schools". Gojendra Verma & Christopher Bagley (eds). *Race and Education Across Cultures.* London: Heinemann, 1975, p. 49.
7. Pollack, Margaret. *Todays Three Year Olds in London* London: Heinemann 1972.
8. Cross, Crispin. Op cit 87.
9. Cross, Crispin. Ibid p. 87.
10. ILEA: Quoted in The Inner City Education, 3rd December 1976 See also Little, A. op cit 13.
11. Driver, Geoffrey. "Classroom Stress & School Achievement" in *Minority Families in Britain.* Khan, U.S. (ed) London: Macmillan Press 1979, pp. 131-132.
12. Little, A. Op cit 17.
13. Townsend, H.E.R. & Brittan, E.M. Op cit p. 135.
14. Cross, Crispin, op cit p. 84.
15. Schools Council. *Teaching English to West Indian Children.* London Working Paper 29, 1971.
16. Cross, Crispin, op cit p. 85.
17. Coard, Bernard. *How the Immigrant Child is Made Educationally Subnormal.* London: New Beacon Books 1971.
18. Little, A.N. *"Performance of Children from Ethnic Minority Backgrounds in Primary Schools".* New Beacon Books 1971.
19. Barns, J. *Educational Priority.* Vol. 3. London: HMSO 1975.
20. Rutter, M.L. et al. "Children of West Indian Immigrants:
    (1) Rates and Behavioural Deviance and of Psychiatric Disorder". *Journal of Child Psychology and Psychiatry 15* pp. 241-262, 1974.
    (2) "Home Circumstances and Family Patterns", *Journal of Child Psychology and Psychiatry 16,* pp. 105-124, 1975.
21. Varlaan, A. "Educational Attainment and Behaviour at School". *Greater London Intelligence Quarterly No. 29,* December 1974.

22. Taylor, J.H. "Newcastle-upon-Tyne: Asian Pupils do Better than Whites". *British Journal of Sociology*. Vol. 54, November 1973 p. 11.
23. Williams, J. *West Indian Children in Dudley Schools*. Dudley: Council for Community Relations 1979.
24. Redbridge CRC. *Cause for Concern: West Indian Pupils in Redbridge*. London. Redbridge CRC, 1979.
25. Driver, Geoffrey. "How West Indians Do Better at School. (Especially Girls)". *New Society*. 17 January 1980, pp. 111-114.
26. Driver, Geoffrey. Ibid.
27. Cross, Crispin. Op cit, p. 86.
28. Driver, Geoffrey. Op cit.
29. DES. *Educational Disadvantages: Perspectives and Policies*. Report of Conference 16 April 1975, p. 9.
30. DES. Op cit p. 7.
31. Driver, Geoffrey. "Classroom Stress & School Achievement" in *Minority Families in Britain*. Khan, V.S. (ed). London MacMillan Press Ltd., 1979, pp. 136-138.
32. Cottle, Thomas, J. *Black Testimony*. London: Wildmoor House 1978, p. 65.
33. Little, Alan. Op cit p. 23.
34. HMSO. *Select Committee Report: Education*. London 1973.
35. CRC. *Teacher Education for a Multi-Cultural Society*. London 1974.
36. Little, Alan. Op cit p. 24.
37. Cross, Crispin. Op cit p. 92.
38. Prince Charles. Report of a speech to Anthropological Institute. London Evening Standard 8 November 1973.
39. Morris, Sam. *Black Studies for History Monograph*. London: Committee on Black Studies 1973.
40. Morris, Sam. Ibid, p. 3.
41. Cross, Crispin. Op cit, p. 93.
42. Scafe, Leslie. Editorial, *Luton Harmony* 1973.
43. Morris, Sam. Op cit, p. 5.
44. Cross, Crispin. Op cit p. 93.
45. HMSO. *Immigrants and the Youth Service*. Report of a Committee on the Youth Service Development Council 1967.
46. Cross, Crispin. Op cit.
47. HMSO. *Immigrants and the Youth Service*. London 1969, p. 8.
48. YSIC. *Youth Service Provision for Young Immigrants,* London 1972.
49. CRC. *Urban Deprivation, Racial Inequality and Social Justice*. London. HMSO 1979.
50. CRC. *Seen but not served – Black Youth and the Youth Service* London 1977.
51. Eggleston, John. *Adolescence and Community: The Youth Service in*

Britain. London: Edward Arnold 1976.

52. Bone, Margaret. *The Youth Service and Similar Provision for Young People.* HMSO, London 1972.
53. CRE. *Youth in Multi-Racial Society: The Urgent Need for New Policies.* London 1980.
54. CRC. *A Second Chance: Further Education in Multi-Racial Areas.* London 1976.
55. CRC. Report of Chief Education Officers. *Funding Multi-Racial Education.* London 1975, p. 3.
56. Little, A. Op cit, p. 25.
57. HMSO. *Select Committee on Race Relations and Immigration.* London 1973. Vol. 1, p. 226.
58. Little, A. Op cit, p. 26.
59. HMSO. *White Paper on Racial Discrimination.* Command 6234 London 1975, para 11.
60. CRC. *Funding Multiracial Education.* London 1975, p. 5.
61. Little, A. Op cit p. 78.
62. HMSO. *Hansard* 4th December 1975, column 2057.

CHAPTER 4

1. HMSO. *Housing Policy Consultative Document.* 1977.
2. Community Roots Resource Centre. *Memorandum on Housing Policy.* London, October 1977.
3. Smith, D.J. *The Facts of Racial Disadvantage.* London: PEP 1976, part three.
4. HMSO. *Census Indications of Urban Deprivation.* Working Note No. 8. London: Department of the Environment.
5. CRC. *Housing in Multi-Racial Areas.* Report of a Working Party of Housing Directors. London 1976.
6. Desai, Rashmin. *Indian Immigrants in Britain.* London: Oxford University Press 1963, p. 43.
7. Cross, Crispin. Op cit, p. 61.
8. HMSO. Circular 33/76 Department of the Environment.
9. CRC. Op cit, pp. 19-20.
10. Pyke-Lees, C. and Gardiner, S. *Elderly Ethnic Minorities.*
11. Smith, D. and Whalley, A. *Racial Minorities and Public Housing.* London. PEP 1975.
12. Smith, D. Op cit.
13. CRC. Op cit, p. 25.
14. Community Roots Resource Centre. Op cit.
15. HMSO. *Council Housing Purposes, Procedures and Priorities.* London 1968.

16. CRC. Op cit, p. 31.
17. "The Hand" is a sort of informal banking club, 20 or so members pay a fixed sum, say £10, to one of the group known as the Banker each week. Each week one of the members receives the full £200. At the end of the cycle it all starts again. Those receiving an early hand in one round drop down in the cycle in the next round. It is also known as "The Turn" or "The Sou-Sou", depending on the island of origin.
18. HMSO. *Race Relations and Housing.* London. DOE, Command 6232 September 1975.
19. Smith. Op cit, p. 286.
20. Rex, J. and Moore, R. *Race, Community and Conflict.* London, IRR 1968.
21. HMSO. Op cit.
22. CRC. *Housing Choice and Ethnic Concentration.* London 1977, p. 12.
23. HMSO. *Inner Area Studies: Liverpool, Birmingham and Lambeth.* London 1977.
24. HMSO. Op cit.
25. CRC. *Housing in Multiracial Areas.* London 1976, p. 11.
26. HMSO. Op cit.
27. HMSO. Op cit, p. 32.

CHAPTER 5

1. Ballard, Roger. "Ethnic Minorities and the Social Services" in minority Families in Britain. Khan, V.S. (ed). London, Macmillan Press 1979.
2. Cheetham, J. *Social Work with Immigrants.* London. Routledge and Keegan Paul 1972.
3. Jones, C. *Immigration and Social Policy in Britain.* London. Tavistock 1976.
4. Triseliotis J.P. (ed). *Social Work with Coloured Immigrants and Their Families.* London. Oxford University Press 1972.
5. Cross, Crispin. Op cit, p. 118.
6. Ibid, p. 119.
7. CRE. *Multi-Racial Britain: The Social Services Response* London 1977, chapter 1.
8. Pyke-Lees, C. and Gardiner, S. Op cit.
9. Hood, R. et al. *Children of West Indian Immigrants.* London: Institute of Race Relations 1970.
10. Moody & Stroud. "One Hundred Mothers". *Maternal and Child Care.*

Vol. III, No. 26, 1967.
11. Pollack, M. op cit.
12. Hunt, Audrey. *Families and Their Needs.* London HMSO 1973 Chapter VI.
13. DHSS/DES. *Co-ordination of Services for Children under Five.* 25 June 1978.
14. Lomas, G. & Monck, E. *The Coloured Population of Great Britain.* London. Runneymede Trust 1975.
15. Cawson, Pat. *Black Children in Approved Schools* London DHSS, September 1977.
16. CRE. Op cit, p. 22.
17. West Midlands Children Regional Planning Centre. *British and Caribbean Born West Indian Adolescent Children in Community Home Schools.* Birmingham 1977.
18. Warren, Peter.
19. Ibid, p. 3.
20. HMSO. *Foster-Care – A Guide to Practise.* London DHSS 1976 p. 44.
21. CRE. Op cit, p. 23.
22. Rack, Phillip. "Diagnosing Mental Illness" in *Minority Families in Britain.* Khan, V.S. (ed). London, Macmillan Press 1979, Ch. 8.
23. CRC. *Who Minds.* London, July 1975.
24. Cross, Crispin. Op cit, p. 129.
25. CRC. *One Year On: The Resettlement of Refugees from Uganda in Britain.* London 1974.
26. CRE. Op cit, p. 42.
27. Baker, Lynda & Husband, Charles. *Social Work Education for a Multi-racial Society.* Unpublished Report. Leicester University School of Social Work.
28. CRE. Op cit, p. 31.
29. Ibid, p. 132.
30. Holman, R. "Immigrants and Child Care Policies". *Case Conference* 1969, 15(7), pp. 255-8.
31. Rea-Price, John. West Indian Immigrants: Assimilation and Casework, *New Society,* 1965, 12(2), p. 40.
32. Fitz-Herbert, Katrine. "West Indians and the Child Care Service" *New Society,* 1967, 9 (239) pp. 604-6.
33. Triseliotis, J.P. "Casework and Immigrants: The Implications of Cultural Factors. *"The British Journal of Psychiatric Social Work"* 1965, Vol. III(I), p. 15.
34. McCullock, M.J. & Kornreich, R. "Black People and the Social Services Departments: Problems and Perspectives" in Brown M.J. (ed) *Social Issues and the Social Service.* London, Routledge and Keegan *Social Issues and the Social Service.* London, Routledge and Keegan Paul, 1974.

CHAPTER 6

1. Foot, Paul. *Immigration and Race in British Politics.* London.
2. Ibid, p. 57.
3. Ibid, p. 59.
4 Ibid, p. 62.
5. HMSO. Hansard, Volume 912, No. 112, column 46. London 1976.
6. Ibid. Column 98.
7 Ibid. Column 86.
8. Ibid. Column 35.
9. Foot, Paul. Op cit 124.
10. HMSO. *Hansard.* Volume 791 No. 11, Column 272/273, London 1969.
11. HMSO, *Hansard,* Volume 906, column 1548, London 1976.
12. Ibid, column 1649.
13. Ibid, column 1606.
14. Rose, E.J.B. et al. *Colour and Citizenship.* London. Institute of Race Relations, 1969, p. 395.
15. National Front. *For a New Britain.* Election Manifesto 1974.
16. *The Economist.* June 2 1979.
17. Rose, E.J.B. et al. Op cit Part II, pp. 43-90.
18. Mullard, Cris. Op cit, p. 49.
19. Smithies, B. and Fiddick, P. *Enoch Powell on Immigration.* London. Sphere Books Ltd., 1969, pp. 19, 20.
20. Ibid, p. 32.
21. Dummett, Ann. "The Real Options on Nationality Law" in *New Society,* November 1, 1979.
22. Ibid.
23. Mullard, Cris. Op cit, p. 52.
24. Rose et al. Op cit, pp. 540/541.
25. Foot, Paul. op cit, p. 221.
26. Rex, John. "The Race Relations Catastrophe" in *Matters of Principle: Labour's Lost Chance.* Harmondsworth Penguin Books 1968, pp. 77-78.
27. Nandy, Dipak. *The National Committee for Commonwealth Immigrants: An Assessment.* London Card 1967, pp. 11-12.
28. Mullard, Cris. op cit, p. 60.
29. Daniel, W. et al. Op cit, p. 81.
30. Hill, M.J. and Issacharoff, R.M. *Community Action and Race Relations.* London. Institute of Race Relations 1971, pp. 286 & 293.
31. Barker, Anthony. *Strategy and Style in Local Community Relations.* London. Runnymede Trust 1975, p. 51.
32. Mullard, Cris. Op cit, pp. 84, 86.

33. Mullard, Cris. Op cit, p. 111.
34. Lane, David. "The Quango . . ." in *New Statesman.* 27 July 1979 page 130.
35. Francis, Kate. ". . . as referee" in *New Statesman.* 13 July 1979, page 130.
36. Lane, David. *CRE Plan 80.* London 1980.
37. Cross, Crispin. Op cit, p. 131.
38. Cross, Crispin. Op cit, p. 23.
39. Ibid, p. 25.
40. HMSO. *Race Relations and Housing.* London 1975, Command 6232, para. 11.
41. CPRS. *A Joint Framework for Social Policies.* London HMSO 1975 para. 11.
42. Mullard, Cris. Op cit 142.
43. NCCL. *Annual Report.* London 1971.
44. Humphrey, D. *Police Power and Black People.* London. Panther 1972.
45. Haynes, A.C.W. *Police Relations with Black Britain.* Unpublished 1979.
46. Banton, M. *Police and Community Relations.* London. Collins 1973.
47. Brown, J. *Shades of Grey.* Bedford. Cranfield Institute of Technology 1977.
48. NYB. *Young People and the Police.* Written evidence to the Royal Commission on Criminal Procedure 1979.
49. Ford, Donald. "Children, Courts and Crime" in *Constable.* London 1975.
50. HMSO. *The West Indian Community.* London, Home Office 1978 Command 7186, pp. 23, 24.
51. CRE. *The Southall Report.* Unpublished report on Southall London 1979.
52 Brown, John. Op cit.
53. CRE. *"Youth in a Multi-Racial Society"* London 1980.
54. HMSO. Op cit 25.
55. Warren, Peter. Op cit, section 3 p. 6.
56. Rose, E.J.B. et al. Op cit, part V.
57. Maxwell, Neville. *The Power of Negro Action.* London, WISC 1965.
58. Mullard, Cris. Op cit, pp. 71, 72.
59. Heinemann, Ben. *The Politics of the Powerless. A Study of the* Campaign Against Racial Discrimination. London IRR/OUP 1972.
60. Mullard, Cris. Op cit p. 140.
61. Dummett, Michael. *Immigrant Organisations.* Unpublished lecture delivered 20th September 1968 to conference of British Sociological Association.
62. CRE. *Participation of Ethnic Minorities in the General Election of October 1974.* London 1975.
63. Ibid, p. 8.

64. Spencer, Richard. *Race Today.* July 1970, pp. 206-7.
65. Anwar, Muhammad. *Votes and Policies.* London, CRE 1980.
66. Ibid, p. 58.
67. Ibid, p. 60.
68. British Council of Churches: *The New Black Presence in Britain.* London 1976, pp. 12-17.
69. Wilson, Amrit. *Finding a Voice.* London. Virago 1978, pp. 168, 171.
70. Mullard Chris. Op cit p. 143.

CHAPTER 7

1. HMSO. *Racial Disadvantage.* London. Home Affairs Committee HC 424-1, 1981.
2. Race Relations Act 1976, Sections 35, 38 set out the general exception under which special needs of prticular racial groups can be met as regards education, training, welfare and ancilliary benefits.
3. Home Office: *The Brixion Disorders 10-12 April 1981.* Report of an inquiry by the Rt. Hon. The Lord Scarman OBE. P. 135. London: HMSO, Command 8427, 1981.
4. Taylor, Wendy. *Probation and After-Care in a Multi-Racial Society.* London. CRE and the West Midland County Probation and After-Care Service, 1981.

BIBLIOGRAPHY

ACDS (Afro-Caribbean Development Society) *Newsletter* Vol. 1, No. 1, September 1977

ACRO (Association of Community Relations Officers) *A Defence Against Centralisation.* London 1971

Allen, Sheila. *Indian Migrants in Britain.* New York: Random House, 1971

Allen, Sheila, Bornat, J. and Bentley, S. *Work, Race and Immigration.* Bradford University of Bradford, 1977

Anwar, Muhammad. *The Myth of Return.* London: Heinemann 1979 *Votes and Policies.* London: CRE 1980

Bainbridge, D. *A Study of the Performance of Pupils of Indo-Pakistan Origins at CSE in a Single Secondary School.* Unpublished Report.

Baker, Lynda. and Husband, Charles *Social Work Education for a Multiracial Society.* Leicester: Leicester University School for Social Work. Unpublished Report

Ballard, Roger. "Ethnic Minorities and the Social Services" in *Minority Families in Britain.* Khan, V.S. (ed). London. Macmillan Press 1979

Ballard, Roger. and Holden Bronwen. "Racial Discrimination: No Room at the Top" *New Society* Vol. 32, No. 654, 1975 "The Employment of Coloured Graduates in Britain" *New Community* Vol. 10 No. 2 1975

Banton, Michael. *Police and Community Relations.* London: Collins 1973

Barker, Anthony. *Strategy and Style in Local Community Relations.* London: Runnymede Trust 1975

Barnes, J. *Educational Priority* Vol. 3, London HMSO, 1975

Bone, Margaret. *The Youth Service and Similar Provision for Young People.* London: HMSO 1972

Brooks, Dennis. *Black Employment in the Black County. A Study of Walsall.* London: Runnymede Trust, 1975

Brown, John. *Shades of Grey.* Bedford: Cranfield Institute of Technology, 1977

Cawson, Pat *Black Children in Approved Schools.* London: DHSS, September 1977

153

Cheetham, J.   *Social Work with Immigrants.* London: Routledge and Keegan Paul, 1972
Social Work and Ethnicity. National Institute Social Services Library No. 43. London, George Allen & Unwin 198

Coard, Bernard.   *How the Immigrant Child is Made Educationally Subnormal* London: New Beacon Books, 1971

Community Roots Resource Centre.   *Memorandum on Housing Policy.* London October 1977
Memorandum on Revision of Section 11 Funding. London 1979
Secretary's Address on the occasion of official opening. July 1978

Cottle, Thomas, J.   *Black Testimony.* London: Wildmoor House 1978

CPRS   *A Joint Framework for Social Policies.* London: HMSO, 1975

CRC   *A second Chance: Further Education in Multi-racial Areas.* London 1976
Funding Multi-racial Education. Report of Chief Educational Officers. London: 1975
Housing Choice and Ethnic Concentration. London: 1977
Housing in Multi-racial Areas. Report of a Working Party of Housing Directors. London: 1976
One Year On: The Resettlement of Refugees From Uganda in Britain. London: 1974
Seen but not Served – Black Youth and the Youth Service. London 1977
Teacher Education for a Multi-cultural Society. London: 1974
Unemployment and Homelessness: A Report. London, HMSO, 1974
Urban Deprivation, Racial Inequality and Social Justice. London, HMSO 1977
Who Minds. London: July 1975

CRE   *Code of Practice in Employment.* London 1980
Five Views of Multiracial Britain. London 1978
Multi-racial Britain: The Social Services Response. London 1977

	Participation of Ethnic Minorities in the General Election of October 1974. London 1975
	The Southall Report. Unpublished Report 1979
	Youth in Multi-racial Society: The Urgent Need for New Policies. London 1980
Cross, Crispin.	*Ethnic Minorities in the Inner City.* London: CRE 1977
Daniel, W.W.	*Racial Discrimination in England.* London: Penguin Books, 1968
Dept of Education and Science (DES)	*Circular 7/65.* London: HMSO, 1965 *Immigrants and the Youth Service.* London: HMSO 1969
Dept of Employment DE	*Gazette.* London: HMSO 1963 "Race Relations and Whites" *Gazette.* London: HMSO 1972
Dept of the Environment (DoE)	*Census Indications of Urban Deprivation: Working Paper No. 8.* London: HMSO 1973 *Census 1971. Advance Analysis.* London: HMSO, 1974 *Circular 33/76.* London: HMSO, 1976 *Council Housing Purposes, Purchases and Priorities.* London: HMSO, 1968 *Housing Policy Consultative Document.* London: HMSO: 1977 *Inner Area Studies: Liverpool, Birmingham and Lambeth.* London: HMSO 1977 *Policy for the Inner Cities.* London: HMSO, June 1977 *Race Relations and Housing.* London: HMSO 1975
Dept of Health and Social Security (DHSS)	*Fostercare – A Guide to Practice.* London: HMSO, 1976 *Report of the Committee of One-Parent Families.* London: HMSO, Command 5629 1974
Dept of Health and Social Security/Dept of Education and Science (DHSS/DES)	*Co-ordination of Services for Children Under Five.* London: HMSO June 1978
Desai, Rashmin.	*Indian Immigrants in England* London: OUP 1963
Driver, Geoffrey.	"Classroom Stress and School Achievement"

155

in *Minority Families in Britain.*
Khan, V.S. (ed). London: Macmillan Press
1979
How West Indians do Better at School
(especially the girls)" *New Society*
17 January 1980

Dummett, Ann — "The Real Option on Nationality Law" in *New Society,* November 1, 1979

Dummett, Michael. — *Immigrant Organisations.* Unpublished lecture delivered 20 September 1968 to conference of British Sociological Association

Eggleston, John — *Adolescent and Community: The Youth Service in Britain.* London: Edward Arnold, 1976

Fitz-Herbert, Katrine — "West Indians and the Child Care Service" *New Society,* 1967, 9 (239)

Ford, Donald — "Children, Courts and Crime" in *Constable* London, 1975

Foot, Paul — *Immigration and Race in British Politics.* London: Penguin 1965

Fox, Derek — *What Ever Happened to the Cullingworth Report.* London: CRE 1980

Francis, Kate — ". . . as referee" in *New Statesman* 13 July 1979

Haynes, A.C.W. — *Police Relations with Black Britain.* Unpublished Address 1979

Heinemann, Ben — *The Politics of the Powerless. A Study of the Campaign Against Racial Discrimination.* London: IRR/OUP 1972

Hill, M.J. and Issacharoff, R.M. — *Community Action and Race Relations* London: IRR 1971

Holman, R. — "Immigrants and Child Care Policies" *Case Conference,* 1969, 15(7)

Home Office. — *Race Relations Act 1976.* London: HMSO, 1976
Racial Discrimination. London: HMSO, Command 6234, 1975
Report on the West Indian Community London: HMSO, 1977
Second Report of the Commonwealth Immigration Advisory Council. London: HMSO, Command 2266, 1964
Select Committee on Race Relations and

	Immigration: 1968-69 Report. London: HMSO, 1969
	Select Committee Report: Education. London: HMSO, 1973
	The Coloured School-Leaver. London: HMSO, 1969
	The West Indian Community. London: HMSO Command 7186, 1978
Hood, R. *et al*	*Children of West Indian Immigrants.* London: Institute of Race Relations 1970
House of Commons	*Hansard* London: London: HMSO, 27 November 1963 London: HMSO, 4 December 1975 London: HMSO, May 1976 London: HMSO, 6 April 1977
HRH Prince Charles	Report of Speech to Anthropological Institute. *London Evening Standard* 8 November 1977
Humphrey, Derek	*Police Power and Black People.* London: Panther 1972
Hunt, Audrey	*Families and Their Needs.* London: HMSO 1973
ICMC	Migration Information Services No. 11
ILEA	*The Inner City,* Education. 3 December 1976
Jones, C.	*Immigration and Social Policy in Britain* London: Tavistock, 1977
Jowell, Roger and Prescott-Clarke	"Racial Discrimination and White Collar Workers in Britain". *Race* Volume XI. April 1970
Lane, David	"The Quango . . ." *New Statesman.* 27 July 1979 *CRE Plan 80.* London 1980
Little, Alan N.	*Educational Policies for Multi-racial Areas* London: Goldsmith College, London University 1978 "Performance of Children from Ethnic Minority Backgrounds in Primary Schools" *Oxford Review of Education.* Volume 1, No. 2, 1975 "The Educational Achievement of Ethnic Minority Children in London Schools" in Gojendra Verma and Christopher Bagley (eds) *Race and Education Across Cultures* London: Heinemann, 1975

Lomas, G. & Monck, E.   *The Coloured Population of Great Britain.*
                          London: Runnymede Trust 1975
Maxwell, Neville.   *The Power of Negro Action.* London:
                          W.I.S.C., 1965
McCulloch, M.J. and   "Black People and the Social Services
Koenreich, R.   Departments: Problems and Perspectives" in
                          Brown, M.J. (ed). *Social Issues and the
                          Social Services.* London: Routledge and
                          Keegan Paul, 1974
McNeal, Julia   "Education" in *The Prevention of Racial
                          Discrimination in Britain.* S. Abbot (ed).
                          London: Oxford University Press 1971
Minority Rights Group   Report No. 23. *Western European Migrant
                          Workers.* London 1974
Mobey, C.   *Social and Ethnic Mix in Schools and the
                          Relationship with Attainment of Children
                          Aged 8 and 11.* London: Centre for
                          Environmental Studies. Research Paper 91,
                          1974
Moody and Stroud.   "One Hundred Mothers". *Maternal and Child
                          Care* Volume III, No. 26, 1967
Morris, Sam.   *Black Studies for History Monograph.* London:
                          Committee on Black Studies, 1973
Mullard, Chris   *Black Britain.* London: George Allen and
                          Unwin, 1973
Mandy, Dipak   *The National Committee for Commonwealth
                          Immigrants: An Assessment.* London:
                          CARD, 1967
National Front   *For a New Britain.* Election Manifesto 1974
NCCL   *Annual Report.* London 1971
NYB   *Young People and the Police.* Written
                          evidence to the Royal Commission on
                          Criminal Procedure 1979
Patterson, Sheila   *Dark Strangers: A Study of West Indians in
                          London.* London: Penguin Books, 1965
PEP   *National Survey of Racial Minorities.*
                          London: 1974
Pollack, Margaret   *Today's Three Year Olds in London.* London:
                          Heinemann 1972
Pyke-Lees, C. and   *Elderly Ethnic Minorities.* London: Age
Gardiner, S.   Concern, 1976
Rack, Philip   "Diagnosing Mental Illness" in *Minority
                          Families in Britain.* Khan, V.S. (ed) London:
                          Macmillan Press 1979